# The Negro and
# Equal Employment
# Opportunities

PRAEGER SPECIAL STUDIES IN
U.S. ECONOMIC AND SOCIAL DEVELOPMENT

# The Negro and Equal Employment Opportunities

## A REVIEW OF MANAGEMENT EXPERIENCES IN TWENTY COMPANIES

## Louis A. Ferman

FREDERICK A. PRAEGER, Publishers
New York • Washington • London

The purpose of the Praeger Special Studies is to make specialized research monographs in U.S. and international economics and politics available to the academic, business, and government communities. For further information, write to the Special Projects Division, Frederick A. Praeger, Publishers, 111 Fourth Avenue, New York, N.Y. 10003.

FREDERICK A. PRAEGER, PUBLISHERS
111 Fourth Avenue, New York, N.Y. 10003, U.S.A.
5, Cromwell Place, London S.W. 7, England

Published in the United States of America in 1968
by Frederick A. Praeger, Inc., Publishers

Library of Congress Catalog Card Number: 68-55003

Printed in the United States of America

PREFACE

In this study, twenty companies were selected for the purpose of observing the application of equal employment practices in company settings and assessing the impact of these practices on minority group employment. Although the selection was not random, the companies represented a variety of employment structures and varied in size, number of branch units, geographical spread and product or service.

The twenty studies cover a broad spectrum of industrial classifications: heavy and light manufacturing; public utilities; service; retail and wholesale trade; and transportation and distribution. All of the companies had publicly pledged themselves to a program of action in equal employment opportunity.

Interviews were conducted with 67 management executives, 27 corporate headquarters officials and 40 management officials in local plants. Interviews were also conducted with union officials in organized companies and two groups of workers--205 white workers, including supervisors, and 215 Negro workers. The observations on these last two samples should be regarded with a note of caution since high nonrespondent rates in both groups undoubtedly resulted in a highly selective rather than representative group.

There are six categories of findings that should be highlighted:

(1) Progress in equalizing opportunities. All of the companies reported some progress in equalizing opportunities, but there was a general feeling among company executives that shortages in adequately trained Negro workers hindered any dramatic change. More accomplishments were reported in developing new procedures in recruiting, relatively few in training and promotion practices. There was more emphasis on developing appeals to skilled Negro workers than unskilled Negro workers. In most companies, relatively little had been accomplished in opening entry jobs to unskilled Negro workers.

(2) Business values and equal employment opportunities. There is clear evidence in this study that a set of values exists in the business community that has implications for the more effective utilization of Negro workers. These values emphasize efficiency of operation and the priority of work standards over equal employment goals, resistance to modifying employment standards to hire Negroes, resistance to increasing Negro job mobility through special quotas for Negroes, and resistance to special employment programs that are not integrally a part of the present employment structure of the company. There is a pronounced tendency to blame

the "inferior" or "different" educational and social background of the Negro for his job difficulties. The Negro job problem is also seen as a community rather than company responsibility. In other words, it is community rather than company resources which must be primarily brought into play to equalize the Negro's job opportunities. There is consensus that management can best act to stimulate community resources to improve the qualifications of future Negro workers. There is repeated emphasis on the belief that whatever management does must be primarily within "normal" employment standards and practices and must not jeopardize work efficiency or production standards. The point was repeatedly made in interviews with local plant officials that an equal employment program must be set within the cost and employment structure of the company and not be an activity in itself.

(3) Satisfaction with Negro job performance. As a group, Negro employees were rated as "average workers" by the management respondents in this study. There were variations in this assessment, however. Negro technicians and professionals were highly regarded, and Negroes in office jobs were viewed as good workers but unwilling to take responsibility. The job capabilities of untrained Negro workers in entry level jobs were not regarded highly.

(4) Union values and equal employment opportunities. With the exception of the Negro membership in two large industrial unions in northern cities, Negroes faced a number of problems both in industrial and craft unions. To a very great extent, these problems reflected union unwillingness to compromise with long-established sets of institutional values--seniority and apprenticeship. A number of industrial unions sponsored activities on a number of levels favoring integration of the Negro into the union, but these still did not give Negroes added leverage in gaining equal job opportunities. The study also suggests that union leaders give relatively little opposition to equal employment practices unless these are in direct opposition to the job rights of white workers.

(5) The white worker's view of the Negro and equal employment opportunities. The following points were apparent in the interviews with whites. First, few of the white workers would admit that Negroes had special job difficulties because of skin color. In the northern plant locations, white workers reported that "Negroes get the same opportunities as anybody else here" but felt that Negroes did not push themselves as hard as whites and had less training. Most white workers were unaware of civil rights issues and were somewhat puzzled that Negroes should be dissatisfied. There was little awareness of specific practices or goals of equal employment programs, and the majority of white workers felt that "special treatment for Negroes" was "not right." The low response rate among white workers perhaps indicated that it was probably the more integration-prone whites who answered the

questionnaires. The response patterns, then, do not reflect the more passionate responses of segregationists. Few of the white respondents believed that a Negro worker should be deprived of the right to a good job if he has the ability, but they felt strongly that he should not get special treatment. As a group, whites reported that Negro workers with whom they worked could hold their own with whites at a specific job. The major fear of whites is that Negro civil rights demonstrations will lead to preferential hiring practices for Negroes and thus limit job opportunities in the company for their own friends and relatives.

(6) The Negro worker's view of equal employment opportunities. In contrast to the whites, the Negro workers felt that there was considerable job discrimination against Negroes in hiring, training and promotions. When Negro job promotion patterns are compared with those of whites, it is apparent that a lower proportion of Negroes advances from entry jobs to more demanding and more responsible tasks. There are some exceptions to this pattern, particularly in two of the electronics firms. One of the major complaints of the Negro worker is that discrimination is subtle. Many of the Negroes felt that they received little help from white workers in informal, on-the-job training or in job know-how that would be valuable for promotion. This latter complaint was particularly frequent among lower skilled blue-collar workers who had received few promotions.

Few of the Negro workers had specific knowledge about the equal employment opportunity program at their company, and fewer knew about agency complaint procedures regarding job discrimination. There was a marked reluctance among these Negro workers to file any complaint, for they felt such actions would make it difficult to continue working at the company or to find employment elsewhere.

As a group, Negro workers felt that their lack of opportunity was more a matter of their skin color than their lack of training. Over half of the Negroes reported that there was a job in the company for which they were qualified by seniority and training but for which they had not applied. The reasons for this vary, but they reflect a certain awareness of hostility in the work environment or lack of confidence that Negroes would be fairly considered for the job.

# ACKNOWLEDGMENTS

It would not be possible to list and thank each one of the individuals who aided me in this research effort. I would like to single out and acknowledge the contributions of the following individuals. First, my appreciation to the co-directors, Ronald W. Haughton and Charles Rehmus, of The Institute of Labor and Industrial Relations, The University of Michigan-Wayne State University. Mr. Haughton was an early advocate of the study and supported the investigation at every stage with wise counsel and untiring effort. The contributions of my graduate staff assistants—David Roth of the Institute of Labor and Industrial Relations at the University of Illinois, J. A. Miller of the Department of Sociology at Michigan State University, and Susan Sheffield of the Department of Sociology at The University of Michigan—should also be noted. The project could not have progressed without the assistance of Robert Manifold and Richard Fogarty, who were my links with the sponsor of the project—the U.S. Office of Manpower Policy, Evaluation and Research (OMPER), of the Department of Labor. They made the administrative and research talents of the OMPER staff available throughout this undertaking.

The manuscript has undergone a number of revisions, and I would like to thank Joyce L. Kornbluh for her efforts in editing and monitoring this work.

Finally, the study would not have been possible without the cooperation of the workers and management and labor union leaders who supplied the information contained in this study.

Louis A. Ferman
May 1968

CONTENTS

LIST OF TABLES

## LIST OF ABBREVIATIONS

EEO-1     Equal Employment Opportunity Form-1

EEOC     Equal Employment Opportunity Commission

MDTA     Manpower Development Training Act

OFCC     Office of Federal Contracts Compliance

OMPER    U. S. Office of Manpower Policy, Evaluation and Research

# The Negro and Equal Employment Opportunities

# INTRODUCTION

Selective buying campaigns, boycotts and picketing; mass protest demonstrations; riots in large urban centers--all of these events have highlighted the dissatisfaction of the Negro with American society. The basic fact is that the Negro is excluded from the mainstream of American life through economic, social and residential segregation. The list of exclusions is numerous, but more and more attention is being focused on the exclusion of the Negro from the world of work. The work role is a primary form of social involvement in our society, determining both the life styles and life chances of individuals. Thus, the quality of the work role and access to decent employment are key data to the understanding of any group's position in and dissatisfactions with the society.

In the present decade, civil rights demands have brought a new awareness of the problems of integrating the Negro into American industry. Although unusual public interest today gives the impression that the origins of equal employment policy are recent, it has had a long history. The fair employment principle was embodied in the legislation of the Great Depression of the 1930's, in which the policy of equal employment opportunity for persons paid from the public treasury was an integral part of the appropriation and enabling statutes dealing with emergency relief. This principle was also affirmed in the work of the President's Committee on Fair Employment Practices during the 1940's and in the establishment of the President's Committee on Government Contracts in 1953.

In the 1960's, the initial thrust in equalizing employment opportunities was in Presidential executive orders. Executive orders 10925 and 11114 provided for the promotion and insurance of equal employment opportunity on government contracts. State legislatures-- twenty-three in all--established state fair employment practices commissions, and, in many cases, this development was supplemented by municipal legislation. On July 1, 1965, Title VI of the Civil Rights Act became operative, banning discrimination in employment in any economic activity. In contrast to earlier periods of our history, equal employment policy in the 1960's was more pervasive, provided for greater implementation by inspection and reporting systems, and emphasized organized, systematic attempts to move minority group members into a key role in the national manpower scene.

Hand in hand with efforts to equalize job opportunities through public policy has been the initiation of a quest to ascertain means and methods of integrating the Negro and other minority group members into American industry. Such knowledge--guidelines for action--was viewed as a key informational resource to all levels of the management community. A number of research efforts were initiated to lay the empirical groundwork for such guidelines. These research undertakings fell into three categories: intensive case studies of companies that already had some experience with equalizing employment opportunities; broad statistical portraits of minority group employment in the community setting; and analysis of minority group employment patterns in leading industries. Each type of study presents data that are necessary for effective public and corporate policymaking.

The first type of study has become a necessary tool for planning action. The case study using descriptive and analytical techniques attempts to assess the underlying dynamics and processes that bring about certain results. Although there are sharp limitations in generalizing the impact of this kind of study, the data are nevertheless productive of hypotheses for further systematic research and insights for policy planning. The discussion in this study is based on the results of such a study, made possible by funding from the U.S. Department of Labor in 1963. The data were gathered in the late summer and fall of 1964.

The changes that have occurred since the completion of the study provide vivid testimony to the changing scene in minority group employment. At the time of the study, there was an inordinate emphasis on intracompany relationships and how they affected equal employment opportunities. Thus, we concerned ourselves with such questions as how corporate decision-makers viewed Negroes and how Negro and white workers viewed each other. Largely under the influence of the Equal Employment Opportunity Commission (EEOC), there has been some shifting of this position to a concern with company-community relationships as a factor in equalizing opportunities. The work of EEOC has also helped focus remedial action on patterns of discrimination in addition to the complaints made by individuals. Thus, the concern has shifted to a consideration of the larger social scene and barriers to employment deeply rooted in the day-by-day activities of institutions.

An excellent example of this new focus are the 1966 hearings initiated by the Commission in the textile industry in South Carolina. In the hearings, information was presented and publicly disseminated on the textile companies (e.g., distribution of the Negro work force), on the economic and social history of the textile industry in South Carolina, on the potential of the Negro work force in the communities where the plants are located, and on recommendations for action to reduce inequities. These public hearings and their published reports provide information on which to predicate change and have become a powerful tool to mobilize public opinion.

There are also a number of other new developments to consider. First, a federal law has been in force since July of 1965 prohibiting discrimination in employment, indicating greater legal pressure for action today than at the time of the study.

Second, at the time of the study, the concept of "affirmative action" was vague and ill-defined. Since that time, both EEOC and the Office of Federal Contracts Compliance (OFCC) have taken steps to clarify the concept. In August, 1966, EEOC presented a series of guidelines for affirmative action in testing procedures, giving some clarity to this area.

Third, Equal Employment Opportunity Form 1 (EEO-1) compliance forms have now been collected for over two years from all employers having 100 or more employees. These data are currently being analyzed in government contract projects at the University of Kentucky and Princeton University. Thus, it is becoming possible to acquire information on the long-range patterns within a company and to study minority group utilization in a particular community or industry over time. The availability of the information itself may become a powerful pressure for improving employment opportunities. Furthermore, the growing emphasis on these data suggests that the problem of minority group employment is being defined differently today from what it was in 1964. Then, the emphasis was on the detection of conscious discrimination practices against minority group members. Today, the more accepted approach is to view minority group employment as a problem of human resource utilization. The marked shift has been from the processing of individual complaints to the identification of, and action concerned with, patterns of discrimination.

Fourth, in 1963-64, the participation of companies in federal manpower programs for the disadvantaged was relatively slight. Since that time, the business community has become more heavily and directly involved with problems of disadvantaged minority groups. This involvement has assumed many forms:   contract management of Job Corps camps; contracts for on-the-job training programs; and voluntary use of instructional and training facilities. In many cases, a more intense and intimate acquaintance with problems of minority group employment has resulted.

Finally, manpower shortages have begun to appear in some job areas, and existing shortages have become more intense. It is obvious that these manpower shortages have improved opportunities for minority group members. In some cases, employment standards and testing procedures have been modified or eliminated to facilitate the recruitment of minority group members into these job opportunities. In November, 1967, the Ford Motor Company began to recruit Negroes in a Detroit ghetto area, almost eliminating the heretofore sacrosanct interview, testing and educational requirements.

At the time of our study, employer emphasis was on the improvement of recruitment procedures rather than on manpower improvement of minority group members in the community. In other words, there was an attempt to seek out the qualified applicant who could meet or come close to meeting company standards. One detects now a slight shift to a concern with minority group employment as one manpower problem of the community that requires unique managerial skills to help upgrade skill potentials. Michigan Bell Telephone Company, a large utility company, has announced the "adoption" of a Negro high school in Detroit, where company personnel will work with schoolteachers and administrators to upgrade the school's technical curriculum and vocational counselling services. A number of other companies have expressed an interest in such a plan. At the time of the study, only one of the twenty companies had taken such a step, and this involved the "adoption" of one-half dozen Negro colleges in the South; company officials and technicians spent furloughs as teachers or administrators to upgrade the school facilities.

Given these changes in equal employment patterns, how valid are the guidelines that were developed in our study in 1964? We believe that these guidelines are still viable and valid for a company that seeks to profit from a review of experiences in a wide range of work situations. An essential element in the development of a sound minority group employment program is administrative practice, and we feel that the principles developed in 1964 can profitably be considered today. We do not intend to catalogue an extensive list of "do's" and "dont's." A body of conventional wisdom has already been developed to cover the basics of equal employment policy; less attention has been given to the subtleties of the administration of such a program. We set the latter as our task.

# CHAPTER 1    THE PROBLEM: DISCRIMINATION IN EMPLOYMENT

The decade of the 1960's may indeed become the most important in the social and economic history of the Negro in America if for no other reason than the remarkable efforts put forth by groups in the public and private sectors of the nation to move the country to accept the principle and practice of nondiscrimination as a Constitutional and moral right of Negroes. These efforts have been made on a broad front: public accommodations, voting, public education, housing and employment. Although there is considerable disagreement on how much progress has been made, it is generally conceded that legal and social aids to equalizing opportunity have been developing at a rapid rate.

This study focuses on one dimension of progress in non-discrimination for Negroes--equal employment opportunities. The data reported are based on observations made of equal employment opportunity programs in twenty separate companies. The questions raised are the following:

1. At the simplest level, how are equal employment opportunity programs organized within a company? What individuals are involved, and what factors influence the content and effectiveness of the program?

2. What are some of the recurring problems in the administration of equal employment opportunity programs? How have these problems been resolved?

3. What are some of the unresolved issues in the application of these programs? What action might be developed to deal with these issues?

To answer these questions, a research design was developed that attempted to isolate the experiences and attitudes of management, Negro and white workers and union officials toward the integration of Negroes into the work force. We were interested not only in the attitudes and opinions of corporate decision-makers but also those of local plant officials and supervisors who were charged with the responsibility of implementing their company's equal employment opportunity program. At every point in the research, we sought to gain insights into the functioning of industrial structures that might have policy or research implications for a better understanding of Negro integration into industry. We attempted to sample--not randomly--situations and structures that could be the basis for hypotheses to be tested in further research. Thus, the goals of this study were concerned more with laying the foundations for further research than with developing definitive statements about equal employment opportunity structures.

The twenty companies represented in this report cover the broad spectrum of industrial classifications: heavy and light manufacturing; public utilities; service; retail and wholesale trade; transportation and distribution.[1]   No claim is made, however, that these companies are wholly representative of all industrial structures in the United States. All of the companies have one important characteristic in common:   They have publicly pledged themselves to a program of action in equal employment opportunity. In some cases, the program is simple in structure with few formal procedures. In others, there is a complex program with formalized procedures. Although the majority of the companies in this study were subject to executive orders 10925 and 11114, some were outside of the scope of these orders and were not subject to them.[2] Many of the companies were included in the Plans For Progress program,[3] but some were either outside of the program or in the process of joining it. An effort was made to obtain a geographical spread of companies in order to compare experiences of similar companies across regions. In all cases, however, the companies did commit themselves to a program of action in equal employment opportunities and did develop procedures to further the program.

---

[1]See Appendix B for characteristics of the companies in this study.

[2]Equal Employment Opportunity in Federal Government on Federal Contracts: Executive Orders 10925 and 11114 (Washington, D.C.: U.S. Government Printing Office, 1963).

[3]Plans For Progress was organized in 1961 and headquartered in Washington, D.C.  The organization was staffed by representatives from business and sponsored by the President's Committee on Equal Employment Opportunity. It sought to enlist companies on a voluntary basis to promote equal employment plans and to aid them in organizing such plans.

## EQUAL EMPLOYMENT OPPORTUNITIES
## IN A COMPANY SETTING

The economic progress of the Negro has been affected by two different kinds of discrimination practiced by companies. First, there is overt racial discrimination, supported by company policy and practice but rarely committed to writing. This may involve intentional restriction of the number of Negroes employed, the assignment of Negroes to traditional Negro jobs or the by-passing of Negroes in opportunities for training and promotion. Second, there may be unintentional discrimination limiting Negro job opportunities, such as in the case of a corporate decision-maker who demands a high school diploma as a requirement for employment or locates the new plant far away from centers of Negro population. To a large extent, intentional acts of employment discrimination against Negroes reflect white attitudes in the wider community, stereotypes of Negro employment and real or imagined resistance by white workers to equalizing employment opportunities for Negroes. The second set of practices--unintentional acts of employment discrimination against Negroes--stems in part from basic mana-gerial assumptions about employment policy and is supported by a logic of operation deeply rooted in the business community. In many instances, this logic of operation does not rest on scientific fact but gains inordinate strength from supporting organizational traditions. This distinction between intentional and unintentional acts of employment discrimination is basic to an understanding of the problems of integrating the Negro into American industry.

The employment policy of any company is viewed by its management as the end product of a rational trial-and-error process by which certain employment activities become accepted as legitimate and need-fulfilling to the organization. To examine or to modify such employment practices is to seriously challenge the company's unique way of "getting things done." For example, the company that relies on new job referrals from its own work force and finds this a successful recruiting practice is apt to resist a change in this practice even if it results in the exclusion of Negroes. Unintentional forms of discrimination are usually linked to employ-ment practices that are viewed by the management as necessary, if not vital, to the firm's successful operation (e.g., vocational testing, recruitment through the private employment agency, etc.). These practices become routinized and beyond question--the "well worn Indian pathways"--and may explain why it is so difficult to reduce forms of unintentional discrimination.

It is an oversimplification to say that all firms practice exclusion or discrimination against Negroes to the same degree. There is a spectrum of discriminatory-nondiscriminatory practices. At one extreme, there are firms unwilling to undertake any remedial

action to change employment policies that are overtly discriminatory. At the other extreme are firms that have made a concerted
effort to examine and eliminate discriminatory practices--intentional
or unintentional--from their employment policy. Most business
organizations fall between these extremes, having an employment
policy that has both intentional and unintentional discriminatory
features.

## The Evidence for Discrimination in Industry

To what extent do firms discriminate against Negroes? The
available evidence, although scanty, suggests that job discrimination is widespread both in the North and in the South. In 1953,
a study of employer practices was made of 1,200 firms in
Pennsylvania. The authors concluded that nine out of every ten
firms practiced some discrimination in hiring, apprenticing and
promoting, with discrimination most prevalent in the skilled and
white-collar occupations.[4]   A review of employment practices in
Ohio in 1958 reached similar conclusions.[5]   A study of minority
group employment practices in San Francisco in 1958 showed
employment opportunities to be widely restricted by race, especially
for Negroes.[6]   The data for other northern areas show similar
patterns.

In the South, the patterns of discrimination are quite clear.
In 1962, Paul H. Norgren undertook a review of employment by
firms in Atlanta,[7] a cosmopolitan city and a rapidly industrializing
urban center. Since these conditions usually favor integration, it
was thought that equal employment opportunities would be more
advanced in Atlanta than elsewhere in the South and might be a clue
to prospects for Negro employment opportunity in other southern
cities. Norgren's observations, however, indicate widespread exclusion of Negroes from employment opportunities in Atlanta in
that year, as the following examples reveal:

---

[4]Employment Practices in Pennsylvania, Report of the
Governor's Commission on Industrial Race Relations (Harrisburg,
Pa. Commonwealth of Pennsylvania, 1953).

[5]Report of the Governor's Advisory Commission on Civil
Rights, Part V, Employment Study   (Columbus, Ohio:   State of
Ohio, 1958).

[6]Irving Babow and Edward Howden, A Civil Rights Inventory
of San Francisco, Part I (Employment Council for Civil Unity in
San Francisco).

[7]The description of racial employment practices in Atlanta is
based on Norgren's data.   See Paul H. Norgren et al., Toward Fair
Employment (New York: Columbia University Press, 1964), pp. 24-27.

(1) One of the automobile assembly plants in the Atlanta area employed 1,700 to 1,800 persons, of whom 70 were Negroes. Only 8 Negroes were employed on the assembly line, 4 having been hired in October, 1961, and 4 in January, 1962. No Negroes held white-collar jobs, and all other Negroes were in low-level service jobs.

(2) A steel mill in Atlanta employed 1,250 persons, of whom one third were Negro. Negroes held no skilled jobs, however, and were confined to unskilled employment at below-average pay rates.

(3) In the construction industry of Atlanta, there were 1,800 carpenters in separate white and Negro local unions. The Negro local had 17 members; the white local membership did the bargaining for them. In 1960, according to census reports, there were 350 Negro carpenters in the area. Apparently, most of them were outside of unions, engaged in free-lance contract work in residential repair. Union membership among electricians totaled 1,200; none were Negro. In general, there were well-developed patterns of Negro exclusion from a variety of other trades--plumbing, sheet metal work and cement finishing.

(4) Negro employment gains were most apparent in all classifications of trucking, warehousing and lumberyards, although Negroes were concentrated within these fields in jobs that minimized contact with whites. Few Negroes held jobs as deliverymen or beer and soft-drink drivers, although many worked as drivers' helpers. In the local transit system, there were two Negro bus drivers and two more in training, but these four were recent additions in previously all-white jobs.

(5) The local telecommunications company employed between 4,000 and 5,000 persons but included only 2 Negro mechanics. All other Negroes employed by the company were in custodial or culinary occupations. With the exception of a few persons, no Negroes were employed in banking and insurance establishments except in traditionally "Negro jobs," save for those employed in the Negro banking and insurance institutions of the city. By and large, Negro employment in retail trade was confined to menial jobs, shipping and delivery. A similar situation existed in the hotel and restaurant industry of the city.

Norgren contends that Atlanta's racial employment practices are typical of the South, with some minor local variations. Collateral studies of racial employment practices in southern communities show approximately the same patterns as in Atlanta. Although a number of pressures for change are apparent in the South--especially in federal contract firms--it is unlikely that substantial changes have occurred since this 1962 study except for token modifications.

## Discrimination and the Employment Process

Discrimination against Negroes--indeed, against the members of any minority group--can occur at a number of points in the employment process: recruitment; selection; placement; promotion; training; and layoff or termination. The forms of discrimination are various and may be intentional or unintentional. It may be well to discuss some of the problems of discrimination at each one of these points as a frame of reference for this study.

## Recruitment

The most obvious form of discrimination is the failure to seek Negro workers for job openings in the company. In some cases, it may be the clear instinct of the management to avoid bringing Negro workers into the company. More frequently, the traditional company channels of recruitment fail to reach Negro workers. Advertisements in white newspapers, recruitment trips to all-white colleges or high schools, the use of private employment agencies and referrals from in-plant personnel may be traditional methods of recruitment that have proved satisfactory to the company in the past but overlook Negroes as a source of labor. Removing discrimination from recruitment requires an expansion of recruitment procedures to reach Negro manpower and a systematic development of confidence in the Negro community that Negro job applications will be welcome. In either case, special recruitment methods must be initiated, and this will mean changes in the resources and activities of the recruitment staff.

Solution

## Selection

Once recruitment channels are open to Negro job-seekers, there is the critical problem of selection. The Negro applicant for a job contends with a number of disadvantages. The first hurdle is the interview. The interviewer may not recognize that the personal indicators of character that he has previously used in evaluating job applicants may no longer be valid when applied to Negroes. Generalizations about job applicants drawn from experience with the white community do not form a suitable frame of reference for the evaluation of a Negro job applicant. From his interviews with white applicants, the interviewer may have a preconceived picture of styles of dress, speech patterns and general patterns of thinking that are necessary prerequisites for the job. Employment may be refused if the Negro deviates from this picture, in spite of the fact that such deviations may be quite normal in his community. The Negro may also be handicapped because he lacks experience with the interview process, experience which the white applicant has usually acquired from his educational and social preparation.[8]

The second obstacle is the testing process. How and why does a Negro perform differently from a non-Negro on employment tests? The answer lies in the tests themselves, as well as in the relative environments. Companies usually set acceptable standards of achievement on intelligence and aptitude tests by correlating the test scores of a large number of their current employees with their levels of job performance. The pragmatic result in a predominantly white company is that the standards have been based on the performance of white middle- and upper-class workers. Therefore, there has developed in these tests a bias that tends to discriminate against working-class and lower-class Negroes.

Two other handicaps faced by Negro job applicants are the lack of appropriate work experience and job requirements. Past difficulties in obtaining meaningful job experience that could be related to the new work situation obviously disadvantage the Negro applicant. It is difficult for a Negro to fill a job opening that requires fifteen years' supervisory experience since few Negroes have had an opportunity in the past to acquire supervisory positions. In a like fashion, many job requirements disadvantage the Negro applicant. Although such requirements frequently reflect outdated thinking about what the job requires, many companies are reluctant to remove or lower requirements, predominantly educational and skill, that would permit many Negroes to become eligible for the job.

Placement

In firms where there is already considerable Negro employment, new Negro employees may be disadvantaged in placement because a tradition of "Negro jobs" has developed. Thus, the placement office may consider the Negro applicant only for those job categories in which Negroes are already employed in great numbers, usually in the unskilled and service classifications. When hiring Negroes for the first time, placement may be made primarily in job categories where white resistance is apt to be minimal. In such cases, the qualifications of the Negro employee are secondary considerations, and underplacement may occur.

---

[8]Kenneth B. Clark, "Clash of Cultures in the Classroom," in Learning Together: A Book on Integrated Education (Chicago: Integrated Education Associates, 1964). See also Frank Riessman, The Culturally Deprived Child (New York: Harper and Row, 1962), and Allison Davis and John Dollard, Children of Bondage (New York: Harper and Row, 1944).

## Promotion and Training

The most obvious form of discrimination in promotion and training is to disregard the Negro as a potential candidate for upgrading or training. The problem is more complex than this, however. It had been established practice in some firms to maintain dual lines of promotion and separate criteria for promotability for Negroes and whites. Thus, in many companies, Negroes have had separate lines of progression that effectively barred them from "white jobs." The qualifications for promotion and training were frequently much higher for Negroes than for whites, and only the most overqualified became eligible.

Two other dimensions of this problem should be mentioned. First, Negroes may not receive the psychological supports from a predominantly white environment to encourage them to bid for such opportunities. As a result, they _feel_ excluded. Second, a great deal of training is informal and depends on the whims of co-workers. Thus, the white worker who is asked to show somebody the ropes-- whether in machine techniques or office procedure--has some discretion in aiding or hindering a Negro co-worker's job opportunities.

## Layoffs or Terminations

Finally, discrimination may be apparent in patterns of layoffs or terminations. Seniority lines may be disregarded to retain white workers during temporary layoffs or permanent cutbacks. Frequently, differential criteria are used to discharge Negro and white workers. There may be a higher tolerance for breaches of company discipline for whites than for Negroes. As a result, the consequences of the same transgression are apt to be more severe for Negroes than for whites within the same company.

In addition, it is also not uncommon, particularly in the South, for "Negro jobs" to be converted to "white jobs" in periods of economic distress when jobs are in short supply. The end result is the frequent termination of Negroes from jobs that they considered "secure."

## EQUAL EMPLOYMENT OPPORTUNITY RESEARCH

Hand in hand with the efforts to give the Negro greater job opportunities through public policy has been the initiation of a quest to ascertain means and methods of integrating the Negro into American industry. The information is scanty, uncoordinated

and largely testimonial. Few vigorous research efforts have tried
to diagnose the elements of resistance and to formulate public
policy to overcome resistance. Much of the existing literature is
"one-shot," with no attempt at assessing the reliability of the
results through replication. Few of the efforts attempt to place the
research into an integrated conceptual framework that can be used
as a starting point for additional research.

There are a number of research traditions in equal employment opportunity research:  the aggregate statistics study; the
descriptive "testimonial" study; and the case study of a particular
plant or industry in which descriptive and analytical techniques are
combined. The literature abounds with the first type of research
project. Statistical portraits give vivid testimony to the existence
of Negro disadvantages and to systematic variations in Negro employment problems. These studies do not , however, specify the
underlying conditions--economic, attitudinal and structural--that
"cause" these problems. At best, such studies portray symptoms,
not causes.

The second type of study--the "testimonial" study--offers
other problems. The main purpose of this type of study is to describe
strategies and techniques that have worked in bringing integration
about in a particular economic unit. The descriptions are usually
from the management's perspective, so that the only problems
discussed are those that infringe on the company's ability to solve
problems. Such studies tell us little about why these techniques have
worked and rarely discuss the problems as perceived from the
Negro or white worker's point of view, or from the vantage point
of the union leader. The third approach--the case study with
descriptive and analytical techniques--attempts to assess the underlying dynamics and processes that bring about certain results.
Although there are sharp limitations on generalizing the results
of this kind of study, nevertheless, the results are productive of
hypotheses and insights for further systematic research and policy
planning. In such a study, numbers are generally made secondary
to an understanding of processes and dynamics. It is this third
approach that will be emphasized in this analysis of the equal
opportunities policies, programs and problems of the twenty companies chosen for review.

Limitations of the Current Study

The present undertaking is not an attempt to catalogue or assess
the total social process whereby Negroes fail to gain access to suitable employment. Employment discrimination against the Negro must
be seen as a process whereby institutional, social and psychological
factors combine at different points during his lifetime to deny
him equal employment opportunities. In adequate prevocational

socialization in the family; inadequate school and housing opportunities; low political efficacy; lack of access to community training
facilities--all of these contribute to the Negro disadvantage in employment. In this study, we are concerned with his access to employment situations, but this emphasis should not mask the larger context
of discrimination.

We could also concern ourselves with how the initial decision
to integrate is made. This is not a primary focus in this study, for
all of the companies have experienced integrated employment for
some time. The emphasis is instead on the methods and problems
of application. The purpose of the report is to instruct companies
that have already made a decision to integrate, rather than to develop a strategy to increase the number of companies with integrated
employment. Information on how the decision was made would provide
valuable insights into the problems of Negro employment, but such
information would be hard to obtain for the twenty companies in this
study, because data would be retrospective, with a number of validity
problems.

## The Chronology of the Research

The study was formally launched in September, 1963, but data
collection did not begin until August of 1964. In the interim, a series
of research instruments, to be described later, were designed and
pretested. Continuous revision was made in these instruments before
the study was submitted to the Bureau of the Budget for clearance.
During this period, the research director and his staff examined
the extensive literature on equal employment opportunity researches,
an activity that had begun six months prior to the project. The intent
was to begin the study in a relatively general, exploratory way and
then move as rapidly as possible toward a systematic and explanatory
investigation.

It had been planned to utilize trained interviewers from the
Survey Research Center of The University of Michigan for the field
interviewing. The majority of the interviewers were from the
Center, but an unforeseen circumstance made it necessary to train
a substantial number of our own interviewers--there was a relative
lack of Negro interviewers in some key locations in the South, where
some of our interview sites were located. It had been decided before
the study to use Negro interviewers to interview Negro respondents
and white interviewers to question white respondents. This decision
seemed reasonable, for we desired to encourage our white respondents to discuss their feelings about Negroes and Negro respondents
to discuss their feelings about whites. We felt that a serious problem
would be introduced by having a Negro interviewer solicit such
information from whites, and vice versa.

Relatively late in the study, we became aware of the community context in equal employment opportunities and made several attempts to solicit information on this variable from local community agencies. The quality of these data was quite uneven, and the data are used in the analysis mainly as reference points.

## The Interview Program

Interviews in depth were conducted with 67 management executives, 27 corporate headquarters officials, and 40 management officials in local plants.  These interviews lasted from 1-1/2 to 3 hours, depending on the extent of equal employment opportunity activities at the company. With the exception of 9 interviews, all of these interviews were conducted by the research director. There were 11 interviews with industrial union leaders and 3 with craft union officials.  Of the interviews with the first group, 7 were conducted by the research director, as were all of the interviews in the second group.

Also interviewed were 205 white workers, including supervisors, and 215 Negro workers. The interviews were conducted by interviewers in the national interviewer network of the Survey Research Center and the specially trained interviewers discussed above.

## The Research Instruments

The decision was made long before the study was undertaken that the primary aim of the inquiry was to solicit a wide range of information on attitudes, behavior and experiences from those individuals who were most directly involved in the work integration process. The various research instruments were designed with this in mind. Let us briefly describe each one of the instruments and its purpose:

Schedule I  This instrument was submitted to the person or persons charged with the responsibility of administering the equal employment opportunity program from corporate levels. In some cases, this individual held the title of vice-president of industrial relations or personnel; in most cases, he was a relatively high official in the personnel department. Twenty-one of the twenty-seven corporate interviews were recorded on a tape recorder and later transcribed.

The schedule was divided into five parts: employment structure and policy of the company; history of the equal employment program within the company; corporate administration of the program; employee recruitment and promotion policies; and grievance and discipline control. With few exceptions, the questions were unstructured and open-ended, designed to solicit frank and informative responses.

Schedule IA      This was a simple checklist of close-ended questions designed to solicit views from corporate officials on the goals of an EEO program within their company.

Schedule II      This instrument was designed to solicit attitudes and expressions of behavior from the local plant officials of the companies being studied. The content paralleled the material in Schedule I, with modifications to account for local plant conditions.

Schedule IIA    This was a twenty-item schedule with checklist and open questions. It was designed to solicit standardized information from local plant officials on topics such as the following: history of Negro employment in the plant; problems--anticipated or real--from equal employment opportunity programs; goals of the program; and sources of Negro recruitment and union structure. This schedule was either completed at the time of the interview, mailed to the respondent for completion or left with the respondent to complete. As originally conceived, the instrument was to be administered through the mails prior to Schedule II, but a number of schedules were not returned on time, and some were lost, necessitating the noted changes.

Schedule III    This instrument combined a number of open-ended and closed questions. It was submitted to the white workers in nonsupervisory positions and to some supervisory personnel. The range of questions was wide, covering such topics as job mobility and training attitudes, knowledge about EEO policy, interpersonal relations at work and images of the Negro worker.

Schedule IV     This instrument paralleled Schedule III but was given to Negroes.  Most of the questions were open-ended. The range of topics included job mobility and training experiences, knowledge about EEO policy and interpersonal relations at work.

Schedule V      This instrument was designed to solicit information on attitudes and experiences of local union leaders on integrating the Negro into the company and the union.

The use of the multiple instruments was justified on three grounds. First, the research was designed to develop an understanding of structures and attitudes associated with the application of an equal employment program.  It was thus necessary to obtain data from a variety of sources. Second, the use of multiple data sources permits a check on the reliability of a single observation. Finally, the use of multiple measures permits a tracing of patterns or trends that would not be permitted by the use of a single instrument.

This is, then, the background of the study. Although we do not have a random sample of integrated companies, the companies in this study have made a public commitment to equal employment opportunities. Thus, their experiences might be viewed for the "possibles" and "not possibles" of equalizing employment. Our investigation should be productive of new insights and hypotheses for further study.

CHAPTER **2** MANAGEMENT EXPERIENCES
WITH EQUAL EMPLOYMENT
OPPORTUNITIES:
RECRUITMENT AND SELECTION

The employment policy and structure of a company are products of both the logic of business efficiency and organizational tradition. In theory, employment policy and practices are designed for the rational recruitment, selection and allocation of workers in the company. The clear intention is to eliminate irrational considerations from intruding at any point in employment decisions and, thus, to promote the greater efficiency of the organization. Employment testing, for example, is designed to objectify job requirements and reduce to a minimum "hunch playing" or personal biases in the selection of a job candidate. We must recognize, however, that tradition may maintain certain employment practices apart from any logic of efficiency. The employment tests that serve in the name of efficiency may be hopelessly outdated or out of touch with the current personnel needs of the company and yet may be maintained by traditional usage. The employment policy and practices of a company must be viewed as the end product of a long trial-and-error process whereby some activities become inscribed with a logic and tradition of their own.

In the recruitment and selection of workers, practices are developed that become part of organization traditions. In recruitment, certain employment channels become highly regarded because they are productive of job recruits. Certain employment aids in recruitment (e.g., the private employment agency) are used and become integral parts of the recruitment process. In a similar fashion, the company develops strategies and techniques for the selection process that are defined as efficient. The development of an equal employment opportunity policy may challenge these practices and necessitate re-examination or revision. For example, a company may be able to recruit all the workers it needs from the referrals of its own work force. For the recruitment of Negro workers, however, such referrals may yield few results. Consequently, it may be necessary to initiate a new series of activities to recruit Negro workers. The old practices must undergo modification or expansion if the equal employment goal is to be met. These changes in employment practices will usually require an additional expenditure of effort and time on the part of the organization.

## RECRUITMENT EXPERIENCES IN
## MINORITY GROUP EMPLOYMENT

The initial development point in an equal employment program is the establishment of recruitment channels to reach the sources of Negro manpower. The structure of such recruiting will be influenced by any and/or all of the following factors: the size of anticipated Negro employment; the kinds of jobs for which Negroes are sought; the number of Negroes already employed, if any, and the kinds of jobs held by these Negroes; and the extent to which Negro applicants are available through traditional recruitment sources. Obviously, the condition of the labor market will also be a factor--the base of recruitment will broaden in a tight labor market and contract in a surplus market.

The recruitment of skilled workers, regardless of their race, is difficult in the tight labor markets that characterize our economy today. On the other hand, the recruitment of semiskilled and unskilled workers is less a problem until a company is faced with the task of converting persons who have been marginal to the labor market into full-time, skilled, productive workers. Additional problems exist in the recruitment of Negro workers who already have some skills or training. Reaching the proportionally smaller number of Negroes who have skilled occupational specialties will necessitate an extensive investment of time, personnel and money on the part of the company as the search is extended to previously untapped manpower sources. A second difficulty in the recruitment of skilled Negro workers is the poor image projected by some companies in their past racial employment practices. Skilled workers in the Negro community may view the recruitment drives of such companies with suspicion and refrain from approaching these companies for employment. A third difficulty lies in the company's lack of experience with and understanding of Negro job applicants--their aspirations and life styles. Although most companies have a thorough understanding of the white job applicant, they frequently find that this knowledge has only partial relevance to their understanding of Negro job-seekers. There is a growing realization that the Negro skilled workers may be interested in a number of employment considerations that do not concern the white worker. The Negro applicant will want information on wages and work conditions, but he also requires information on supervisor-Negro relations in the company or the handling of Negro grievances. It is necessary for the recruiting staff to learn more about Negro life styles, especially as they bear on employment.

Some problems are also presented in recruiting less skilled Negroes for break-in jobs--clerical, production and service. The educational achievement levels of the Negro manpower pool in the United States is lower than that of whites and, even in cases where achievement is equal, the low quality of education in predominantly Negro schools leaves the Negro job applicant lagging behind the white in a number of skills--verbal, mathematical and social. Recruitment of these workers may involve the question of compensatory education or training to raise their employment potential.

There is no doubt that for many companies, the recruitment of Negro job applicants involves a whole new range of activities and value assumptions not necessary in the recruitment of white workers. Furthermore, a meaningful recruitment program for Negroes will involve organizational costs in time, personnel and money not encountered in the recruitment of white workers. For a number of reasons, however, the strategy for the recruitment of white workers has only limited application to the recruitment of Negroes, and a company that does not provide for the difference will undoubtedly encounter difficulties in recruiting Negro employees.

With these introductory remarks, we will turn to a consideration of some summary statements on recruitment of Negro workers and then detail some of the experiences and problems observed in the twenty companies that confirm, negate or modify these propositions. They are not intended as dogmatic principles of application but rather as frames of reference or guidelines for the consideration of minority group employment. While it is true that each company develops distinctive solutions to its minority group employment problems, each company may borrow--and hopefully profit--from the experiences of other companies.

## The Cycle of Recruitment

Two basic trends in recruitment of minority group workers are discernible in the twenty company histories of equalizing employment. First, there is a sharp change in the structure of recruitment when employment philosophy moves from a "nondiscrimination policy" to a "policy of affirmative action." In the former case, the company makes nondiscrimination in employment an established policy of the company and makes public acknowledgment of this fact. No special efforts are made to reach out to the community to recruit Negroes, and it is assumed that public awareness of the policy is sufficient to draw Negro applicants to the company. In an affirmative action program, practices are initiated to make special efforts to open channels of recruitment to Negroes and, in some cases, to develop special programs to make trained Negro job-seekers available. Sophisticated understanding of minority group recruitment problems quickly brings a realization that a nondiscrimination policy without affirmative action fails to stimulate the recruitment of Negroes.

A second basic trend is the movement of companies through a series of stages in the recruitment of Negro workers--first, a reliance on personal contacts in the Negro community or a random search through Negro clubs, churches and associations; second, a reliance on contacts and associations with formalized job-finding structures in the Negro community (e.g., Urban League, Negro college placement office); and third, a reliance on the Negro employees of the company to suggest referrals. It is obvious that considerable Negro employment must occur before the third stage develops. Although we can speak of a stage development in Negro recruitment, the activities in each one of the stages can, and frequently do, coexist. It seems clear from our interviews that corporate officials and local plant personnel officers seek to "normalize" Negro recruitment by moving toward the use of the same employment channels for Negroes and whites. The use of informal contacts and formal agencies of the Negro community are perceived as extraordinary methods in the initial stages of recruitment. The use of referrals from already employed Negro workers and direct solicitation from Negro applicants are viewed as a more permanent, normal way of doing things.

The sum of experiences in the twenty companies indicates that a nondiscrimination policy by itself does not result in increased numbers of applications by Negro job-seekers. Only a small proportion of Negro job-seekers may be aware of the policy, and an even smaller proportion may apply for jobs. In some cases, Negroes may suspect the company's motives in public expression of a nondiscrimination policy, especially if the company's past employment practices have been discriminatory. In other cases, the Negro applicant seeks information and assurance that the work environment of the company is not hostile. For these reasons, the company must reach out into the Negro community rather than wait for the Negro job-seeker to come to it.

There are a number of levels, ranging from the impersonal to the personal, at which contact between the company and the Negro community can be established. These contacts function to meet a variety of needs both for the company and the Negro job-seeker. The company obtains a network of referral sources for job applicants, as well as access to information on Negro life styles, job aspirations and job-hunting patterns. These contacts may increase the Negro community's confidence that the company is serious in its nondiscrimination policies. For the Negro job-seeker, these contacts provide information about job openings, offer access to an equal employment opportunity job channel and give some assurance that the company desires to employ Negroes.

Such contacts may be established through Negro-oriented advertising in the mass media, shared sponsorship of activities in the Negro community, membership of company executives in Negro associations or action groups and/or informal personal contacts with key leaders of the Negro community. The pattern of contact will vary from company to company, reflecting the values of the company as well as the organization of Negro life in a given locality.

## Mass Media Contacts

The use of mass media advertising as a device in recruiting Negroes is quite common. Such advertising may make a direct or indirect appeal. The simplest use of the direct approach is the designation of the company as "an equal opportunity employer" in employment advertising. A common device is to sponsor employment ads in journals or publications that cater to Negro subscribers. Indirect approaches include using Negro models in product advertising in the press or television and pictures in company publication outlets or trade journals showing Negro employees in responsible jobs in the company or in contact situations with top executive leaders. Both approaches may be of some value in creating a favorable mood for Negro employment but are rarely effective in and of themselves in increasing the flow of Negro job applicants. To be effective, mass media contacts must be complementary to a range of more personal contacts. Based on the experiences of the companies in our study, the following guidelines would seem to apply to mass media contacts:

(1) Mass media contacts should not be restricted to Negro publications or channels of communication. The vice-president of a large manufacturing firm reported that Negroes suspect tokenism when the company avoids equal employment opportunity ads in predominantly white newspapers. His own company was cited for tokenism by a Negro action group when product advertisements with Negro models were prominent in Negro publications but did not appear in the large metropolitan newspapers read by whites.

(2) Mass media contacts must be reinforced by affirmative action on the part of the company. The use of the mass media is largely symbolic and should not be considered as a substitute for more intensive forms of recruiting activity in the Negro community.

## Shared Sponsorship of Activities

A number of companies have supplemented mass media contacts by sponsorship or co-sponsorship of community activities directly linked to the recruitment of Negro workers. Most of these activities are designed to link the company to a wide variety of associations that touch potential job applicants and create a favorable image of the company. These activities include "career days" and job clinics for disadvantaged youth, work experience programs following school hours, guidance seminars for vocational counselors in Negro schools and shared sponsorship of job orientation or placement programs with Negro agencies (e.g., the Urban League).

These activities have been initiated to deal with four problem areas in company recruitment of Negroes: personal motivation in job aspirations; job information; strengthening of educational resources in the Negro community; and job training. In 1963, a large, eastern manufacturing company became concerned because few Negro job applicants had been attracted to the company by newspaper ads. Consultation with officials of the local Urban League indicated that few Negroes in the area had sufficient information about potential jobs in the company and that their aspirations for jobs lagged behind expanding opportunities with the firm. The company organized a five-point program designed to increase the motivational and information level of Negroes in three target areas of a large metropolitan area:

(1) A speakers' bureau offered lectures to high school and civic groups on opportunities within the company, its growth potential and changing technology.

(2) A semiannual career day, co-sponsored with fifteen companies in the immediate area was initiated, and regular job clinics were made available to high school youth after school classes.

(3) A series of visits to the main plant were planned for Negro youth, including as part of the visit extensive orientation on machine procedures and the division of labor in the plant.

(4) An individual counseling program was opened in the local Urban League office for resident Negroes.

(5) A series of meetings with eight to twelve Negro families-- parents and children--was planned at which were presented, through the use of lecture or visual aid material, profiles of new job opportunities for Negroes, the qualifications for these jobs and information on the company's nondiscrimination policy. In one location during the six months following the initiation of the program, the company had 630 Negro job applicants. Interview data indicated that 598 of the applicants became interested in the company through some phase of this program.

An aerospace firm on the West Coast has an identical program, and it has produced similar results. In this firm, a summer work experience program was undertaken for Negro youths still in high school who were paid regular wages and were distributed throughout thirty-five of the plant's ninety-four departments. The personnel director felt that the work experience program has a twofold benefit. The youth could be retained on a "look and see" basis for future job applications and would also be able to give their classmates a realistic appraisal of job opportunities and conditions for Negroes in the plant.

A leading electronics company was faced with a critical shortage of technicians. Projected trends indicated that the shortage would continue for some years because competitive recruiting was draining some of the better sources of referrals. The company decided to tap some new sources for recruitment--the southern Negro colleges. An early appraisal found few of the southern Negro candidates capable of passing the entrance qualifications. The company initiated a four-point program in fifteen southern Negro colleges. As a first step, several training administrators spent some time in the colleges reorganizing the curricula in mathematics, physics and engineering, where it was found that the curricula, teaching methods and materials were out of touch with the realities of a modern technological system and the job requirements of large companies. Secondly, the company lent its specialists in physical science subjects to a number of colleges to enrich the instructional staff and conduct an informal program of job counseling for upperclassmen. Summer work programs for selected faculty members from these colleges were initiated at a northern production center, where an attempt was made to upgrade the teacher's technical knowledge and familiarity with the job market requirements of new technological systems. Finally, the company initiated a work experience program for qualified students during the summer period. The company perceived these activities as a long-term program and plans to expand its activities to other campuses. After the first year's operation, fifty Negroes from these colleges accepted employment with the company in scarce technical categories.

Several companies have co-sponsored training programs for Negroes or racially mixed groups in clerical and stenographic skills that are in demand in the labor market. In a large eastern city, a private college organized a special stenographic course for forty-five job-seekers, thirty of whom were Negro. Seven companies sponsored the program, agreeing to pay the tuition as well as to employ qualified graduates. On completion of the course, a work experience and course performance summary was developed for each candidate and circulated to the personnel departments of the sponsoring companies. All but two of the course participants were placed.

A program for twenty-five vocational counselors from predominantly Negro schools was co-sponsored by sixteen companies in a large midwestern city. It had been evident for some time that Negro youths at these schools were inadequately counseled about requirements and job opportunities in the labor market. A five-week, full-time session was conducted for these counselors in a local college. Officials from the state employment service and vocational education system, as well as representatives from the co-sponsoring companies, detailed trends in the immediate labor market, discussed equal employment legislation and the changing requirements for jobs and emphasized the changing employment patterns for Negroes. As an inducement to attend, the companies paid the salaries of the counselors and pledged sufficient funds to pay the tuition costs for advanced graduate study for three of the group recommended by the instructional staff.

Three conclusions would seem to be suggested:

(1) The shared sponsorship of activities must be on a broad front and attempt to deal with some of the major deficiencies of the Negro communities (e.g., job information, prevocational training). These activities should be need-reducing rather than symbolic.

(2) Programs must be developed independently for each community to deal with the basic problems in that community. Caution should be used in adopting a program in a community solely because it has been successful elsewhere.

(3) There is a danger in attempting to change aspirations without correlative change in the opportunity structure. A firm in the Midwest initiated a strong stay-in-school campaign in the Negro community, promising potential employment to high school graduates from a predominantly Negro school. However, only 14 of a class of 165 could qualify for employment on the company's test battery. About the same proportion of high school dropouts were successful applicants, pointing to the poor quality of the educational institution and casting doubt on the validity of the high school diploma as an indicator for employment in Negro communities.

## Executive Membership in Negro Associations

The membership of key boards, committees and social action groups in the Negro community offers another important contact between company and potential Negro recruits. Several companies have recognized the importance of such memberships and have systematically encouraged their executive personnel to undertake such activities. A large utility in the Midwest requires that executives initiate such activities in their own community and that a record be kept of such contact situations. This company has emphasized that such activities are important considerations in evaluating top executives for promotion. A more common event is the voluntary participation of a top company executive in the activities of a Negro organization. Such memberships serve a number of purposes for the company. For all levels of company workers, such memberships become symbolic commitments on the part of the company to the employment of minority group members. This is particularly true when the company gives extensive public acknowledgment of such memberships and when the executive is a person of high standing in the company. For the Negro community, such memberships are a symbol of the company's interest in the problems of Negroes and its willingness to invest its time and resources to help in their solution. The executives themselves are given an opportunity to obtain firsthand knowledge of the problems and life styles of the Negro community and can channel this information into company programs for minority group employment.

The following points should be noted about such contacts. Given the network of groups and organizations in the Negro community, it is frequently difficult for a single executive to share in the activities of more than a few groups. It is always a recurring question whether these limited associations are productive of a range of experiences that will result in potential recruits for the company from the Negro community. There is also a danger in overidentification with a single group or organization with consequent loss of confidence or charges of tokenism by other segments of the Negro community. One manufacturing firm has attempted to solve this problem by encouraging a number of executives to participate in Negro activities and organizations. Regular bimonthly meetings are held in the company headquarters to collate these experiences into a composite picture of the Negro community. Two basic guidelines should govern such contacts. First, they should be widely distributed throughout the Negro community, making every effort to establish working relationships with a wide range of groups and organizations. Second, the activities of the executive must be more than symbolic in orientation. In many instances, the involvement of company executives in Negro community organizations is a new event and one marked by suspicion and charges of tokenism by segments of the Negro community. Contacts characterized by short-term involvement in superficial issues feed these suspicions.

## Informal, Personal Contacts

A number of companies have gone beyond the secondary, impersonal contacts described above and have attempted to form a close personal relationship with key members of the Negro community. These contacts have been in a number of directions. In one case, groups of ten to twenty people have been invited to lunch at the plant with personnel department officers. Following the luncheon, there has been a tour of the plant and an orientation session explaining job requirements, company nondiscrimination policy and company recruitment practices. Another company has established the practice of having personnel officials in all its branch units make personal contacts with key Negro community leaders. Personnel executives have established contacts with each one of eight Negro ministers in a community within the state, regularly attend Negro churches and have initiated small luncheons with key Negro community opinion-makers. Seven of the companies in the present study have employed Negroes in their personnel departments for the principal purpose of establishing close contact with leaders in the Negro community. The range of contacts is quite extensive and includes Negro teachers employed in the school system, Negro faculty members of colleges or technical institutes and Negro ministers. Through their Negro employees, two companies participate in the affairs of Negro women's clubs, which are a good source of referral for white-collar workers. An executive of a large manufacturing company has cultivated the acquaintance of Negro scout leaders, welfare workers and recreational workers who have an extensive acquaintance with Negro youth and, therefore, are excellent sources of referrals.

Undoubtedly, such personal contacts yield many applicants who could not be reached through traditional job-referral channels. However, while fulfilling a need in the minority group employment market, personal contacts as a source of referrals may offer some disadvantages. The executive of a large electronics firm reported that such contacts were valuable but that few good job applicants resulted from them. He felt that Negro leaders had only a vague notion of the job requirements in his company since few of them had had any extensive experience with company employment. Consequently, few of the referrals from ministers or business leaders were hired by the company; they lacked necessary skills or educational requirements for job vacancies. The experience of this company has been contradicted, however, by the experiences of a number of other firms. While admitting that many referrals were not adequate, the companies cited numerous instances where referrals for clerical or service jobs had been hired. It would seem that, as a general rule, the value of informal contacts in recruitment lies mainly in the referral of job applicants for nonprofessional and non-technical jobs rather than for more specialized employment.

There are two other common problems associated with informal contacts as a means of recruitment in the Negro community. First, there is the tendency to view the Negro community as a homogeneous grouping to be reached by contact with a small number of leaders. Such a picture obscures the considerable diversity of Negro life and may result in personal contacts with a very select segment of the community. Second, there is a pronounced tendency for these contacts to be established with clusters of individuals in the upper- and middle-class strata rather than with low-income groups. The result is that Negroes from the former groups become favored job-seekers while little help is available to the low-income population, which needs the contacts most. A company official from a large public utility found that his company has established few ties to low-income groups in the Negro community in spite of an excellent record of contact with more affluent groups. Under the urging of the company personnel director, a number of personal contacts were initiated with the ministers of store-front churches, directors of settlement houses and neighborhood block club leaders of low-income areas. These contacts yielded a number of applicants for service, production and clerical jobs in the company.

These observations about the establishment of ties between the company and the Negro community deserve comment. The value of these contacts is twofold. They create a mood or climate in which the Negro job-seeker can determine the relative seriousness of the company effort to hire Negroes; and they provide a source of job information to Negroes who may have few other communication channels to the company. It is difficult to evaluate the efficacy of any one kind of contact for recruitment. This will depend to a large extent on the organization of the particular Negro community. As a rule, such contacts should attempt to sample a wide variety and number of experiences, values and attitudes in the Negro community. Consequently, the establishment of ties with the Negro community will involve a coordinated effort entailing all four of the contact situations described above.

The contact pattern between the company and Negro community is strikingly different in southern than in northern plant locations. Regional differences do not eliminate the need to establish such contact but do point to differences in the way that contact is established and maintained. In the South, there is more reliance on personal contacts with Negro leaders and individuals for job referrals while avoiding ties to Negro action groups. Two factors may account for this. First, Negro action organizations (e.g., NAACP or Urban League) are concentrated in the large cities, and there are few branches in small communities to use in recruitment. A second reason is also likely. Membership of company executives in Negro action groups is usually frowned upon in the South. It may result in community pressure on the company officials who, consequently, may avoid extensive public displays of nondiscrimination policy and transmit job information to Negroes on a more restricted basis through personal contacts with key members of the Negro community.

## Community Agencies and Recruitment

Specialized Negro agencies play a considerable part in the recruitment of certain categories of job applicants. Such agencies may fulfill a number of functions in the recruitment process. Through its members, they may act to locate job applicants, an activity that is costly and time consuming when undertaken by the members of a company personnel department. Such agencies may also screen the job candidates and assemble test data, personal employment histories and general employment information. It is also possible that the agency can create a more comfortable climate for screening job applicants by mediating the recruitment process between job-seeker and company. A Negro may find it less threatening to accept employment refusal by staff members of a Negro agency than by white officials in the company personnel department.

A review of the experiences of the companies in our sample indicates frequent use of Negro organizations as aids in the recruitment of Negro job candidates. The Urban League operates a series of regional skills banks which serve both Negro job applicants and companies that seek Negro job applicants. For each candidate, there is a detailed work history and record of past training. Brief summaries of the qualifications of each candidate are sent to inquiring companies on request. A company with no particular job in mind may receive a list of applicants or may solicit a candidate with particular skills to fill a specific job vacancy. Although there is some variation in practices among the regional skills banks, the emphasis throughout the units is on a rational organization of the minority group labor market both for job applicants and the company. The bulk of job applications and placements are in the clerical specialties. Some companies have enlarged the activities of the Urban League skills banks in their areas by conducting intensive training programs for job counselors employed by the agencies. A large electronics company has undertaken to train job counselors in the local skills bank and in other Negro agencies who can then screen potential job applicants for the firm. The job counseling program emphasizes the personnel techniques used by the company to screen job applicants and describes standards and qualifications acceptable to the company. In effect, the skills bank functions as an extension of the company personnel department, and recommendations for employment by the skills bank staff are closely followed by the company. Another company in a midwestern state has initiated the practice of lending job counselors to a number of Negro groups in the area in order to screen job applicants before they enter the formal screening channels of the company. The vice-president of the company felt that this practice reduced recruiting costs and provided a psychological setting in which potential job candidates could feel comfortable in the recruitment process. In a large midwestern city, a Negro agency has initiated the practice of inviting potential employers to interview prospective job candidates in the agency offices, thus giving the applicant an opportunity to explore the job market in a more organized fashion and the company an opportunity to meet a number of job candidates in a single setting. A large eastern manufacturing company initiated a program for the chief officers of Negro action groups to discuss and analyze cooperative methods of recruiting minority group members. This company also developed a similar program for department heads of local offices of the state employment service.

It is obvious that such Negro agency activities can and do play a large part in organizing the labor market for a segment of the Negro community. The Negro agency has a market advantage in locating job applicants through its familiarity with problems and target groups in the area. It can reduce certain organizational costs in recruitment for the company by performing a number of activities that would entail considerable cost in time, money and effort for the personnel department. For the job-seeker, it offers a channel to employment opportunities that he could not acquire without a considerable investment in time and effort and a well-developed structure for job-seeking.

As noted earlier, informal relationships with the Negro community dominate in the early stages of a recruitment program. Some of the disadvantages of referrals from informal sources can be mitigated in a shift to referrals from specialized Negro agencies or organizations. The company can rationalize its recruitment procedures by objectifying the requirements for a job. Paper procedures eliminate some of the trial-and-error, intuitive aspects of referrals through informal contacts. The Negro agency frequently employs scientific procedures of screening applicants, based on familiarity with the technical requirements of jobs in certain employment classifications. In some cases, the Negro agency may conduct a study of specific job requirements in a particular company. In screening applicants, the agency makes a thorough rational assessment of the candidate's capacity to fulfill these requirements. Thus, considerable time and effort may be saved by a company that can utilize the services of an agency that specializes in the placement of minority group membership.

### Recruitment and New Channels of Job Referrals

The recruitment of Negro workers for professional, clerical and technical jobs will often require the exploration of new sources of job recruitment. The executive respondents in our study were almost unanimous in agreeing that trained Negro workers were in short supply and were generally not accessible through traditional channels of recruitment. They indicated that intensive recruitment efforts were under way in two relatively new sources of job applicants, the predominantly Negro high school and the southern Negro colleges. There has also been an increasing use of newspaper ads in Negro publications and some contact with employment agencies that specialize in Negro job applicants.

The local plant officials in our study were queried about effective sources of recruitment for white and Negro workers. The data in Table 1 indicate that recruitment sources of Negro job-seekers are different in a number of respects from those of whites.

Referrals from company employees and direct applications-- the two major sources of white workers--appear to be less important as effective sources of recruitment of Negroes, although they were mentioned by some respondents. The most striking observation is the company dependence on Negro agencies as a source for referrals. It may well be that the more qualified Negro applicants seek the placement services of Negro agencies, or are sought out by such agencies, rather than solicit employment directly. The agency network may indeed be a crucial consideration in recruitment in the period before the company has sufficient Negro employees to refer job-seekers directly to the personnel department.

## TABLE 1

### EFFECTIVE RECRUITMENT SOURCES FOR WHITE AND NEGRO WORKERS REPORTED BY RESPONDENTS IN TWENTY LOCAL PLANT UNITS[a]

| White Workers | Negro Workers |
|---|---|
| Direct applications (20) | Urban League, NAACP or other Negro agencies (18) |
| Informal referrals from workers or other employers (18) | Referrals from Negro employees (16) |
| Visits to high schools or colleges (17) | Negro colleges (12) |
| Referrals from employment agencies--public or private (10) | Negro newspaper and magazine ads (10) |
| Newspaper ads (2) | Visits to Negro high schools (10) |
| | Direct applications (8) |
| | State employment service (7) |
| | Referrals from Negro churches or settlement houses (4) |

[a]Figure in parentheses refers to the number of plant officials who designated item a major source of recruitment. Twenty companies designed "direct application" as the major recruitment method for whites, and eighteen designated Negro agencies as the major sources of Negro recruitment. The maximum number in parentheses is twenty.

The data in Table 1 do not tell us the most effective sources of referral for different kinds of Negro workers. It would seem likely that Negro technicians might be in different recruitment channels than Negro semiskilled workers. The respondents were asked, "Which of the referral sources would you say has been most effective in recruiting the following groups of Negro workers-- trainees in management program, white-collar workers, technical workers, lower-skilled workers?" The responses to this question are tabulated in Table 2.

TABLE 2

EFFECTIVE RECRUITMENT SOURCES FOR GROUPS
OF NEGRO WORKERS REPORTED BY
TWENTY LOCAL PLANT UNITS[a]

| Management trainees | White-collar workers |
|---|---|
| Negro or white colleges (18) | Direct applications (17) |
| Negro agency referrals (14) | Referrals from Negro |
| Referrals from Negro com- | leaders or in- |
| munity leaders or in- | fluentials (16) |
| fluentials (10) | Negro agency referrals (16) |
| Direct applications from | Newspaper ads (2) |
| workers at other | |
| companies (5) | |

| Technical workers | Lower-skilled workers |
|---|---|
| Negro or white colleges (18) | Direct applications (20) |
| Negro agency referrals (17) | Referrals from workers (17) |
| Technical institute place- | |
| ments (8) | |
| State employment service | |
| referrals (4) | |

[a]The figure in parentheses refers to the number of plants that
considered item an effective source of recruitment.

These data indicate that the recruitment of highly skilled personnel
is primarily through Negro or white colleges with some aid from
Negro agencies and influentials. By way of contrast, white-collar
and lower-skilled workers are recruited largely through direct
application, although Negro agencies and leaders also exert some
influence on the job-finding experiences of white-collar workers.
These observations reinforce our earlier conclusion that recruitment
of Negro workers requires special activities on the part of the
company, particularly in locating new sources of referrals and developing contacts with segments of the Negro community.

## SPECIAL PROBLEMS IN THE RECRUITMENT OF
## MINORITY GROUP WORKERS

There is no doubt that the recruitment of Negro workers, particularly in the skilled occupational categories, presents a number of problems to business organizations. There was almost unanimous agreement among our executive respondents that two problems in particular loomed large. There was a lack of qualified and trained Negroes for existing job vacancies; and Negro job candidates were not in the usual channels of recruitment. These problems, it was reported, were also made more intense by the strong competition for trained Negro workers that characterizes the current labor market.

The solution to these problems necessitates a new range of activities by most companies. The first is the enlargement of the channels of recruitment to institutions in the immediate Negro community: high schools with large numbers of Negro students; Negro agencies that specialize in minority group employment problems; and the Negro colleges in the South. These institutions must be incorporated into the recruitment schema of the company, not simply as emergency or temporary sources of recruitment, but as normal channels of locating workers.

It is also necessary to undertake a systematic review of the practices in the traditional channels of recruitment. Frequently, referral agencies may have Negro job candidates but may exclude them from consideration because of tradition. In a southern city, the state employment office servicing a transportation manufacturing company had not referred registered Negro job applicants for production jobs because there was an expectation that such jobs were open only to whites. In a midwestern city, the vocational counselors of a large high school did not refer Negro youth for mechanical jobs in an electrical manufacturing company because there was considerable doubt concerning their acceptance into union membership, a condition of employment. In cases where the company has limited control over the channels of recruitment, as in some union contracts or arrangements with private agencies, such exclusion practices may exist almost without notice. The recruitment of Negroes into the company will necessitate forceful actions on the part of the company to curb such practices in these organizations.

The special problems in recruiting Negro workers can be classified under four headings: underqualification; residential location of Negro workers; job mobility patterns of Negro workers; and preferential treatment for Negroes in recruitment. Let us consider each one of these in turn.

Underqualification and the Recruitment of Negro Workers

All of the management respondents reported that the chief
problem in recruitment was the underqualification of the Negro job
applicant. There was agreement that this underqualification was
the result of past inequalities of opportunities, rather than an innate
biological inferiority of the Negro. The most frequent objection to
Negro job-seekers was that few of them had the necessary educational
requirements, usually a high school education, to be employed by
the company in break-in jobs. It was also reported that large numbers of Negro job-seekers with high school diplomas had not shown
adequate mastery of verbal and mathematical skills to qualify for
employment, a condition resulting from inadequate preparation in
predominantly Negro high schools. There was also widespread
agreement that in order to find one qualified Negro, an inordinately
large number of Negro applicants had to be screened. A plant
manager in a midwestern manufacturing firm reported that only
1 out of every 15 Negro applicants showed potential for hiring,
and a manufacturer of office equipment reported that 113 Negro
girls had been screened to fill 4 office jobs. Almost all of the local
plant interviewees agreed that the ratio of applicants to hirees
was more favorable among white job-seekers than among Negro
job-seekers. This suggests two possibilities. First, the number
of Negro applicants with adequate requirements is low compared
to the total number of Negro job applicants, a charge made repeatedly by our management interviewees. Second, a more intensive screening process exists for Negroes, and, thus, more Negro
applicants are screened to find the select few. There was no direct
evidence in our interviews to support the second possibility, but
it is likely that both factors are operating in the recruitment of
Negro workers.

A second handicap of Negro job applicants was the lack of
specialized training for a job. In some cases where the Negro did
have the specialized training, there was a lack of special tools
or legal license to perform the job. An electrical equipment firm
in the South contacted two Negroes who had a background of training
in electrical work but did not employ them because they lacked a
state license for such work. An automotive repair company located
a qualified Negro mechanic, but he lacked the necessary tools for
the job. There was a tendency on the part of some companies to
modify requirements for skilled jobs, especially if these deficiencies
could be remedied by on-the-job training. However, the modified
requirements for entry into skilled jobs varied considerably and
was certainly not a consistent practice. A large electronics company desired to employ 86 technicians in 3 new plant locations.
A review of available manpower showed that few job applicants had
the necessary qualification--a high school education with 2 additional
years of technical school. The company undertook to modify the

requirements on a trial basis. Accepted for employment were 23 applicants with 6 months of technical school. These workers were required to attend a company training program that compressed 18 months of technical school training into 7 months. The program was conducted concurrently with a work experience program in the shop. At the end of the school period, the work performance of the graduates was evaluated against the work performance of workers with the regular qualifications. The profiles were almost identical. Consequently, the company has modified its requirements for the technician jobs. A midwestern retail store lacked job applicants possessing the required skills for stenographic work. The company employed 15 girls in clerical jobs closely related to the stenographic work. As a condition of employment, the girls were required to attend 2-hour afternoon classes in stenographic skills and 1 weekly evening session. The training was conducted on the company premises, using company equipment and instructors. All but 2 of the girls were transferred to stenographic work at the completion of the training period. These examples indicate that marginal job applicants can be utilized by a company if three conditions are met: a realistic reappraisal of the qualifications of the job; the development of a training program to meet these new qualifications; and the providing of job-related employment for a temporary period until the new skills are acquired. Although such programs have been the exception rather than the rule, they offer a unique opportunity to utilize the manpower of the underqualified job applicants.

A third measure of underqualification of Negro applicants was the high rate of rejection based on medical deficiencies. The executive of an electrical manufacturing company indicated that 3 out of 5 Negro applicants could not pass the entrance medical examination. The vice-president of a steel-processing firm reported that the firm had undertaken to employ long-term unemployed Negroes in a large metropolitan area for available unskilled and semiskilled jobs. Of the 1,200 Negroes who were screened, only 97 could pass the entrance physical. It was reported that almost one half of the job applicants had medical ailments that needed remedial attention before employment was possible.

Finally, some Negro job applicants were considered underqualified because they apparently lacked career potential. This group of applicants were considered to be adequate for break-in jobs, but the hiring personnel had some doubt about their ability to progress and build a career in the company. In a large national chain of retail stores, the assumption in hiring full-time employees in break-in jobs is that they possess potential to become a managerial staff member of the store. Applicants are rejected if the company feels that they lack such potential. Apparently, underqualification must be judged in terms of the assumptions made about hiring, employment and career in a company.

## Residential Location of Negro Workers

The spatial segregation of Negroes into urban and rural ghettos has a marked impact on their employment opportunities. The decentralization of industrial activity from the large city into the regional hinterland increases the distance between home and work place that must be traveled by the Negro worker. Some employers show a marked reluctance to hire job applicants who commute from a considerable distance since they may not be able to be punctual during periods of inclement weather, and the worker's efficiency is reduced by their heavy investment in travel to work. The job-seeker, Negro or white, attempts to minimize time-away-from-home and is apt to avoid seeking jobs that are too great a distance from home. Plant managers in the study, particularly in small towns, felt that difficulties in hiring Negroes were intensified when there was a small Negro labor market in the local community and a considerable distance to large centers of Negro population.

The recruitment of Negroes, it was reported, is also made more difficult by restriction of good housing opportunities in the local community. The personnel director of a large southern plant attributed the inability of his company to employ Negro professional and technical personnel to local community practices of exclusion in housing opportunities. It was apparent to this respondent that, in looking for employment, Negro professionals give considerable attention to community traditions in minority group opportunities for housing, recreation, education and community participation. An aggressive vice-president of a small electronics company in the Midwest organized a concerted effort to provide good housing opportunities for Negro technicians who had recently joined the company. He made personal contact with local real-estate agencies, church groups and civic leaders. Six of the ten Negro technicians employed in the company found good housing in the community. Apparently, the success of the vice-president in finding housing was related to two factors. There had been no tradition of Negro residence in the community, and the Negroes involved were in high-status jobs, similar to those of their white neighbors. In a second community with a long history of low-income Negro residences, this same company had little success in finding good housing for three Negro technicians. Several companies operate house-finding services for new employees but have had little success in changing prevailing housing patterns for Negro workers. There is a tendency for most of these services to accept community norms in housing and attempt to place new Negro employees in sections of the community designated as "Negro housing."

The residential "ghettoization" of Negroes has another consequence. Ghetto life may generate a sense of psychological security, if for no other reason than it represents the familiar. The manager

of a large transportation company reported that it was difficult
to recruit Negro technicians or secretaries if the job involved
leaving the area of residence. This respondent also reported that
it was difficult to recruit Negroes as salesmen to travel from city
to city. The expressed preference had been for employment in
proximity to the Negro community. Another executive from an
electronics company indicated that Negroes expressed a desire to
avoid placement in communities without substantial Negro residence,
although the expansion of the company had been largely into small
communities with few indigenous Negro residents. It is obvious that
this residential immobility of Negroes may contribute substantially
to a self-restriction of opportunities.

### Job Mobility Patterns of Negro Workers

Negro job applicants may be recruited from a number of other
sources. The manpower pool that would seem to offer potential job
recruits of proven quality is the Armed Forces and government
service. A rigid merit system in both services has resulted in the
development of a large number of trained and skilled Negro workers.
In seven of the companies in this study, some attempt had been made
to recruit from this pool. The results were generally poor. Although
salaries in business were better, few of the Negroes chose to leave
a career in the Armed Services or government to accept employment
in private industry. The reason may be twofold: a high investment
in a seniority and retirement system; and a reluctance to leave a
familiar situation with considerable guarantee for merit employment. A large retail store chain had more favorable experiences in
the recruitment of retired military personnel. A Negro major
accepted an executive position in the president's office, and an
army master sergeant became a buyer. It may also be possible to
recruit from among Negroes employed in other business organizations. The skills banks of the Urban League are concerned with
unemployed workers but also actively attempt to increase the mobility
of Negro job-holders by making them aware of new openings in a
number of business organizations.

### PREFERENTIAL TREATMENT OF
### NEGROES IN RECRUITMENT

While preferential treatment in recruitment is rejected in
principle, some companies have adopted various forms of preferential
treatment in practice. Usually, acceptance of preferential treatment in recruitment has been temporary and the result of urgent
pressures for change in the company's employment profile. The
management executives in our study recognized the possibility of

preferential treatment in a number of recruitment practices, but only a few of them fit the recruitment experiences of the companies. Three major practices will be discussed. Although they may be regarded as preferential treatment they can be considered in a broader context as remedial measures: quota setting; designating certain jobs to be filled by Negro job applicants; and broadening recruitment to include employee prospects in Negro high schools and colleges as well as those registered with Negro agencies.

### Quota Setting and Recruitment of Minority Group Workers

As a group, our management respondents rejected the practice of setting quotas for Negro recruitment. It was clear, however, that most of them accepted the idea of "targets" or "goals" for increasing Negro employment. Thus, in eleven out of the twenty plants, the management had set a goal of increasing Negro employment to a point that the proportion approximated the percentage of Negroes in the local community. In a large electrical equipment company with plants across the country, a target system for recruitment has been developed. Each plant situation is examined, and targets for Negro employment are set. Dates are established by which these targets are to be met, and progress is audited by an examination of bimonthly reports. As a target is met, a new one may be established. The number of Negroes to be hired is influenced by the size of Negro population and the availability of a variety of skills in the local Negro labor market. In turn, each plant is expected to establish appropriate targets for each one of its divisions or departments. This procedure has significantly increased Negro employment in this company. In several instances, the local plant managers have developed on-the-job training programs to upgrade the skills and employability of Negro job applicants. These programs have largely resulted from the pressures to find skilled Negroes to meet the employment targets. The company places the burden on each local plant manager to find or develop qualified Negro employees to fill the goal. A second company has developed a quota system whereby a certain number of Negro job candidates are required to be interviewed for employment. The number is set sufficiently high to insure that the recruitment staff will be exposed yearly to a large number of Negro job applicants.

While quotas are rejected outright in most northern plant locations, the concept of proportional hiring existed as part of implicit employment policy in two southern plants. In one location, a 10 per cent goal had been set, and the plant manager in a second had established that Negro employment approximate the percentage of adult Negroes in the community. Quota setting apparently has greater legitimacy in the South than in the North and is accepted as a "normal" procedure. The concept of racial balance appears as a value in most major southern institutions, and the business organization is no exception.

Designating Certain Jobs To Be Filled by Negroes

A second form of preferential treatment is to designate a certain number of jobs to be set aside for qualified Negro applicants. There was considerable emphasis on "qualified," and all management respondents were opposed to hiring underqualified Negroes for token representation in certain categories of jobs. The practice of an East Coast company is illustrative. The president of the company ordered that, as a remedial measure, 25 per cent of all new job openings in the company would be set aside to be filled by qualified Negro job applicants from the outside. If a qualified Negro could not be hired immediately the job would remain open until such an applicant was found. The responsibility for locating an acceptable applicant was shifted to the head of the department. The plan was given extensive publicity in the press and did result in opening a number of all-white departments to Negro job applicants. There was apparently little resentment among white workers, but serious objections were voiced by the local union president, who felt that the seniority provisions of the union's contract had been compromised. The president of the local NAACP also objected. He felt that this practice might cause considerable white-worker resentment and increase the difficulties in hiring Negroes. The practice has since been modified and is now confined exclusively to jobs outside of the union bargaining unit. A second company in a large southern community has also set aside a number of key jobs to remain open until filled by Negro job applicants. In other companies, there has been a practice of holding open a small number of key jobs until qualified Negroes can fill them. In the latter cases, the goal is to make a breakthrough into traditionally white jobs, rather than to appreciably increase Negro employment.

This strategy is most apparent in the early stages of an equal employment opportunity program. Its value is not in increased Negro employment, but, in establishing Negroes in key jobs in the company. The strategy also has the advantage of limiting the flexibility of a local plant decision-maker in filling jobs, thus curbing traditional prejudices in recruitment.

Broadening Recruitment

A third strategy is to broaden the company's sources of recruitment, giving particular emphasis to sources where Negro job candidates can be found. A majority of the companies in our study have shifted to intensive recruitment in Negro high schools and colleges. In one case, the personnel director of a large electronics firm reported that, in 1964, company recruitment was de-emphasized in white high schools and overemphasized in Negro high schools to increase the number of Negro job applicants for the company. Our respondent indicated that this was a temporary adjustment in recruitment practices to correct an imbalance in the company employment profile. He felt that the prospects at the Negro high school met fewer of the company's requirements for employment but that these deficiencies could be corrected by on-the-job work experience and company-supported remedial programs in the local high school.

## SELECTION EXPERIENCES IN MINORITY GROUP EMPLOYMENT

After locating a job applicant with apparent qualifications for employment, the company must decide whether or not to hire him. There are a series of reference points used in making this decision: employment testing of various kinds; a personal interview; recommendations from trained vocational counselors; letters of recommendation from former employers or school teachers; and, in some cases, an investigation of the applicant's background. For most nonmanagerial jobs in the company, the major reliance is placed on the interview and employment testing. The battery of tests may contain both personality and aptitude inventories, but, for nonmanagerial job-seekers, the use of personality assessment tests is infrequent, and the main instruments of assessment are aptitude inventories.

For Negroes, the interview and employment testing may present formidable barriers to employment. First, the Negro's attitude toward these methods of assessment may be such as to induce hostility and resentment with consequent withdrawal of the job application. For many Negroes, the testing is perceived as a method of denying the Negro an opportunity for employment. It is frequently seen as a devilish device to reinforce a not-to-hire decision that the corporate decision-maker has already reached. In this context, the test is apt to arouse suspicions and dampen motivation. Another familiar problem with the interview and testing is the difference in background between the tester and the job applicant. There is no doubt that many assessment devices have been developed around white middle-class norms familiar to the tester but outside the stream of experience of the job applicant. The style of dress and speech mannerisms exhibited in the interview situation and the applicant's inability to deal with certain concepts in the tests may be viewed as handicaps for employment by the tester and yet be understandable in the context of the applicant's life style. The crucial question is whether such "handicaps" really offset job performance. The experiences of the tester preclude rational judgment of how these differences may affect job performance.

The tendency, however, is to regard them as "handicaps" because they do not fit the pattern established by white job applicants.

Third, many tests are used as rites de passage rather than as a rational assessment of ability. In many companies, the tests are outdated, demanding test performance in no way related to the actual job requirements. The test validity, if established, reflects national norms rather than the demands of the local job situation. For some companies, the tests are organizational traditions rather than devices to assess potential performance on specific jobs.

Quite apart from resentment, the interview or test may induce considerable anxiety in Negro job applicants. The phenomenon of "clutching" in tests is more common among Negroes than among whites. In the segregated school, the tradition of education has not favored the development of sophistication in interviewing or testing. For many Negroes, these are relatively new experiences with no clear definitions or guidelines. Furthermore, some of the employment testing situations may recall school testing situations in which the candidate may have been less than successful.

One final point should be mentioned. There is considerable variation in the purposes of testing. In one company, testing may be used to assess the job applicant's career potential with the company; in another company, it serves to assess his trainability potential; in yet another company, it functions as a measure of potential performance on a specific job. The assessment device may offer problems for Negroes as well as whites; more than competence for a particular job is usually being evaluated.. Low scores on the test may deny the Negro applicant employment not because he lacks potential for a given job but, rather, because he lacks career potential. In many cases, the significance of the test results can only be seen in the total context of assumptions that the company makes about hiring and employment.

Some companies recognize these problems in the selection process and are reluctant to depend on any one assessment measure for a final hiring decision. In the more sophisticated firms, testing and the interview are two of a number of indicators that are collated for a total assessment of the candidate.

## The Interview Situation

Three basic factors enter into an interview situation: the values of the interviewer; the context in which the interview is conducted; and the attitude of the job applicant toward the interviewer. The interviewer may consciously or unconsciously harbor prejudices against the job applicant and indicate this to the job applicant by verbal or behavioral cues. More difficult to isolate is an unconscious rejection of a job candidate. The interviewer who may vehemently deny that he has any prejudice may still be affected by the applicant's style of dress, speech, handwriting on personnel forms or pre-interview experiences. In turn, the applicant may be cowed by the physical aspects of the interview situation, or the interview may be too short to assess the potential of the candidate. Finally, there may be strong feelings of resentment or suspicion of the interview situation based on previous negative experiences or unfamiliarity with the interview process.

The failure of a company to recruit large numbers of Negro workers may be partially attributable to the attitudes and behavior of corporate decision-makers and their unit subordinates who are the gatekeepers of the company. The latter group in particular is in a strategic position to foil even the best-developed nondiscrimination plan. These company employees represent the company to job applicants and can intentionally or unintentionally influence the company decision to hire the applicant as well as the applicant's decision to accept or refuse employment in the company. The key factor in successful recruitment of Negroes may well be the extent to which the attitudes and behavior of this group can be controlled. At the outset, these workers must be convinced that the company nondiscrimination policy is more than a statement of principle and that the company is fully serious about implementation. The extent to which this is done will be a direct reflection of the commitment of corporate decision-makers to the policy.

A number of practices have been developed to deal with this problem. First, it is possible to arrange for the education of these workers on the issue of minority group discrimination. A large national electronics company undertook a five-point program of education for local plant managers and staff-recruitment workers (interviewers and vocational counselors). An intensive three-day seminar was initially held at corporate headquarters, bringing together educators, leaders of Negro action groups and long-service Negro employees. Considerable emphasis was placed on a discussion of Negro life styles, the nature of discrimination and employment problems of minority groups. A second phase included a discussion of how stereotypes intrude in the recruitment process and presented specific case material. This was followed by small group discussions on issues and problems in the recruitment of minority group workers with special attention to individual experiences. A fourth stage involved group meetings which discussed specific problem cases.

In the fifth and last stage, an audience-participation meeting, a panel of long-service Negro employees detailed their experiences and expectations in the company. Using representatives from this session to help them, the company officials duplicated this effort at thirteen of its largest facilities. There have been efforts in other companies to influence the behavior of the employees directly involved in the recruitment of workers, but none has been as ambitious as the above program. In other companies, these efforts have emphasized traditional personnel training techniques in brochures and lectures by supervisors. All of these efforts stress equal employment opportunities as a sound personnel practice rather than as a moral issue.

A second practice designed to influence the behavior and attitudes of subordinates engaged in the recruitment of Negroes is the development of an audit system. In one manufacturing company, recruitment interviewers must detail their contacts with Negro applicants in a special report. They must indicate the qualifications of the Negro, the jobs that were considered for him, the disposition of his application and, if rejected for employment, the reasons for rejection. This procedure was initiated to protect the company against legal action by rejected applicants but has developed into an instrument through which decisions by subordinates can be examined. In a second company, no formal records are kept of rejected applicants, but interviewers must be prepared to defend their decisions in writing. In both of these cases, upper-level executives are charged with responsibility for auditing, giving the activity an aura of importance in these companies. Finally, one of the most practical techniques is to have the executive officer of the company communicate with these subordinates in writing. The content of the message varies, but, in form, there is a restatement of nondiscrimination policy and an exhortation to implement this policy in practice. Because some evasions of policy may stem from a lack of awareness as to how top executives feel about the policy, the communications may have some influence. Although these techniques can minimize evasions of the policy, they probably do not completely eliminate discriminatory attitudes and behaviors, which are, to some extent, a reflection of personality needs and socialization.

## The Structure of Interviewing

The structure of the interview situation can also be changed. Several companies, recognizing that many Negroes do not show to their advantage in a single interview situation, have adopted the convention of multiple-session interviewing for minority group candidates. The Negro job applicant may be brought back a number of times to gain a better picture of his abilities. Another strategy is to locate the interview situation away from the company. In a southern-based company, Negro job applicants have been interviewed in neighborhood churches and in the offices of Negro action groups. The same practice has been followed in a number of northern locations. This approach should be offered as an option and not as a practice, for it would be easy to interpret this practice as an attempt to avoid bringing Negroes to the company location, a charge made against one of the companies in a southern location. Still another strategy is to make use of Negro interviewers or Negro action groups to conduct the initial interview and act as intermediary between the applicant and the company. Such a decision, however, must be on an individual basis, since many Negroes are quite sophisticated in handling interview situations due to experiences in the Armed Services or in previous employment.

A recurring question in the interviewing of minority group workers is the potential usefulness of Negro interviewers in the personnel department. There was considerable disagreement among our executive respondents as to whether Negroes should be used to interview Negroes and, if so, how they should be used. The argument in favor of Negro interviewers stresses that Negro applicants feel more comfortable with a Negro interviewer since they can obtain information on racial practices in the company and community, a topic that would not be openly discussed with a white interviewer. The argument against Negro interviewers is that the practice bears the stamp of tokenism and is embarrassing to the interviewer and the applicant. The Negro applicant might well interpret this practice as a company style of "treating Negroes differently." One company has initiated the use of mixed teams of Negro and white interviewers. The job applicant sees both members of the team together on the initial contact and then separately as the occasion demands. The executive officer of this company feels that the team system is especially appropriate in visits to Negro or white colleges in giving job applicants some indication of the level of job responsibility of Negroes in the company. Although the use of Negro interviewers for Negro job applicants was popular in the mid-1950's, current practices utilize Negro members of the personnel department for interviewing in general rather than confining them to interviewing Negro applicants.

## The Attitudes of Job Applicants

Although Negro attitudes toward interviewing and testing are important factors in the selection process, relatively little has been done to change this dimension of minority group employment. One company on the West Coast has worked with the state employment service to make pre-employment counseling available to Negro job applicants. This counseling involves a number of trial test situations in which old test forms of the company are submitted to the Negro job-seeker. Members of the company personnel department explain the purpose of the tests and discuss the structure of the items. The employment service has also initiated a series of prototype interview situations in which the Negro job-seeker is counseled on manner, dress, grooming and interview behavior. In a large midwestern city, a private Negro organization has worked with a group of companies to conduct counseling sessions for Negro job applicants. The main aim of the program is to familiarize the Negro with the structure of tests and their meaning. These programs

are exceptional; only one of the companies had continuous involvement in such activities.


## EMPLOYMENT TESTING EXPERIENCES IN
## MINORITY GROUP EMPLOYMENT


The role of employment tests in minority group employment
has been the subject of considerable debate. Those who oppose testing as an assessment tool in minority group employment muster
the following arguments. First, the norms for most tests are developed on the performance of white workers, usually middle-class,
making it difficult for Negroes from other social environments to
pass them. The discrimination against the Negro in testing is not
based on skin color but rather on differences in class. Second, tests
are frequently used with no validation for job performance, raising
the possibility that some Negroes could perform the job well, test
scores to the contrary. Third, the tests assume a level of education
found in a smaller proportion among Negroes than among whites.

Those who favor testing make the following points. An employment test objectifies job requirements and puts the question of hiring
on an objective basis, rather than depending on the subjective whims
of the corporate decision-maker. In this context, the tests are a
means of insuring nondiscrimination in hiring. A second argument
in favor of testing is that it is a short, economical way to assess
the potential for adequate job performance. The argument is also
presented that test profile results can given an indication of the
intellectual strengths and weaknesses of the minority group candidate and can be used for remedial work. Finally, it is argued that
the test provides a better indication of ability than any other assessment tool, be the candidate white or Negro.

There is still another possibility. Tests may be unfair to the
Negro because many operating personnel have an insufficient knowledge of testing theory to understand the use of employment tests.
Tests are usually based on national norms and yet are used to
assess the potential performance of a local work force. Of the
companies studied, only a few have attempted to establish local
performance norms for the tests. The tests frequently gauge the
test performance of Negro job applicants against a national norm
rather than against the performance norm of the local work force.
Very often there is failure to provide systematic follow-up studies
to determine if the tests are measuring potential job performance
accurately. Usually, the only guide to the soundness of the tests is
line department satisfaction or dissatisfaction with the performance
of workers who have achieved satisfactory test scores. Few attempts
have been made to study workers who have high test scores but do
not perform well on the job or whether rejected job applicants could

perform well in the work situation if given a chance.[1] Such information could reduce manpower costs and provide for more efficient hiring practices. Nevertheless, in many situations, the particular test is retained on the basis of traditional usage or because the tests have proven themselves efficient in other companies with advanced personnel methods. Quite frequently, the rational basis for the use of a particular test is difficult to find, although admittedly the right test can appreciably improve the selection process.

Some of these difficulties in testing were recognized by our management respondents. As a general rule, there was more sophistication in testing theory among corporate respondents than among local plant personnel. As a group, our management respondents felt that test scores in and of themselves should not be the sole basis for hiring. The test should be one of a number of considerations in selection. Test scores apparently serve as an initial selection device rather than as a final criterion for hiring. It is possible for a job applicant to pass the battery of employment tests and not be hired, but rarely are workers hired who do not pass the tests.

One final point should be mentioned. There is considerable variety in the kinds of employment tests used by companies and in the length of time such tests are used without revision. A large distribution firm has used a simple twenty-two item mathematics test for break-in job applicants for twenty-one years without revision. The test was developed by a company vice-president, and the use of the test has been traditional. One company subscribes to a national testing service and receives the latest testing devices as they are developed. The use of tests in employment selection varies from company to company, and it would be difficult to understand the role of the tests in minority group employment without some understanding of the history of testing in a specific organization and the values assigned to this procedure.

## Testing and Preferential Treatment

To what extent should a company give minority group members preferential treatment in testing? This question has generated considerable controversy in recent years. It has been proposed that Negroes be given some preferences in hiring to make up for past

---

[1]In one of the local plants studied, fifteen Negro workers were employed on a production line in assembly work. Due to production pressures, these workers were hired without the usual Wunderlicht battery of tests. After a six-month period, the workers were given the tests. In spite of the fact that each one of the workers had received a satisfactory supervisor rating on the job, not one of the fifteen received a passing test score!

disadvantages. This preference in tests might be developed in any one of three ways. First, Negroes might be exempted from such tests. The argument is that since Negroes do poorly on the tests, and since in many cases we do not know if the tests really assess job performance, the selection of Negroes should be made on a basis other than testing (e.g., interviewing). The second method would be to hire Negro applicants if they missed a passing score by a few points. As in the case of veteran preference in civil service, a fixed number of points would be added to the Negro's test score. The third possibility would be to hire the Negro job applicant regardless of test score and arrange for some form of compensatory education on the job. Finally, the company could also give preference to the Negro job applicant whose test score was identical to that of a white candidate.

In principle, the management respondents rejected the concept of preferential treatment in testing. The main arguments were that such preferences undermined the rationale for tests and that white worker morale would be adversely affected. In practice, however, there were some notable examples of preferential treatment. In the hiring of clerical and technical workers, a number of companies have given Negro job applicants preferential treatment if their test scores were comparable to those white applicants. This practice is generally in evidence when the company is anxious to change its minority group profile as a response to civil rights pressures. A large electronics company has adopted the convention of employing Negroes on a trial basis even if their scores were slightly below the accepted standard. This is not an absolute practice but exists on an individual case basis. Exempting Negro job applicants from testing or giving preference to an underqualified Negro candidate, particularly when a qualified white candidate is available, is not an accepted practice but has occurred in initial attempts by a company to change its employment profile or to meet the objections of a federal compliance review.

It is difficult to generalize on preferential treatment practices. The essential consideration is how anxious the company is to change its profile or fill a personnel need and how much value is placed on hiring Negroes in certain job categories. Under these pressures, exceptions are made, but preferential treatment hardly becomes a general rule. Preferential treatment is generally confined to those cases where the Negro applicant has done as well as the white applicant.

### Testing and Pre-employment Investigations

In certain companies, part of the hiring process involves a pre-employment investigation of the applicant. Although the evidence is meager, the results of such investigations can offset adequate test scores and result in refusing the applicant for employment.

The vice-president of an aerospace firm noted that a review of hiring practices in the company revealed that employment decision-makers generally placed more reliance on the data in these investigations than on test scores in hiring. The results of such investigations may particularly disadvantage Negro job applicants who have been employed in marginal jobs or have changed jobs frequently. One company official noted that if the pre-employment investigation showed a record of arrests, the candidate would be rejected, no matter how well he did on the test. Again, the Negro applicant is disadvantaged; since the brutality and violence of his environment frequently involve him with the police, justifiably or not. It is clear, then, that performance on testing batteries is frequently evaluated in a larger context of applicant inspection and may particularly disadvantage Negro job applicants.

CHAPTER **3** MANAGEMENT EXPERIENCES
WITH EQUAL EMPLOYMENT
OPPORTUNITIES: PLACEMENT,
TRAINING AND PROMOTIONS

The nondiscriminatory employment policies of the companies in this study extended beyond statements of principles on the recruitment and selection of minority group workers. There was a concern with other dimensions of the employment structure: placement; training; and promotion. As in the case of recruitment and selection, considerable variation existed in these three areas in the companies' experiences and practices, making it difficult to formulate summary statements equally applicable to all twenty companies.

The main organizational principle underlying placement, training and promotion is that workers with potential or demonstrated abilities and capacities should be given opportunities impartially, free from any other considerations. The major aims are to utilize the employment assets of any job-holder and to reduce to a minimum the underutilization of any employee.

In reality, however, certain conditions may combine to deny to even the most promising worker certain job openings, advancements or training. There are at least seven factors that can contribute to the underutilization of the minority group worker even after he is recruited and selected for employment: stereotypes of Negro abilities or job capabilities; stereotypes of customer or co-worker reaction to working with Negroes; traditional patterns of job assignment for Negroes and whites; reticence of Negroes to bid for nontraditional job assignments or training; departmental supervisory flexibility in job assignments and placements; informal pressures and hostilities in the work environment; and overqualification and underplacement in job assignment. Let us briefly discuss each one of these in turn:

(1) Stereotypes of Negro abilities or job capabilities. The most obvious limitation on Negro job placements, training and promotion is the stereotypes of Negro capabilities held by corporate or local plant decision-makers. These may range from a very general hostility toward the Negro worker ("He is lazy, shiftless, and ignorant.") to some very specific notions of his limitations

50

("Negroes cannot stand office discipline," "Negro workers cannot stand heights," "Negro workers can stand heat better than white workers."). The origins of these stereotypes are usually lost in the socialization and background experiences of the decision-makers. These stereotypes frequently exist where there is a lack of real acquaintance or contact with Negroes and are susceptible to modification when the decision-maker engages in personal contact with Negro workers. There is an obvious circularity here insofar as the stereotypes impose a limitation of contact that, in turn, further reinforces the stereotypes.

(2) Stereotypes of customer or co-worker reactions. Another restriction on Negro job assignment is management anticipation of the negative reactions of customers or white co-workers to Negro placement. The desire to avoid an unpleasant situation frequently causes hesitation in assigning Negroes to nontraditional jobs (e.g., sales or white-collar). Two errors of judgment are usually apparent. First, many management decision-makers fail to understand the extent of contact that has already occurred between whites and Negroes. His white workers and customers may have had extensive contact with Negroes in the Armed Services, in school or in previous employment, making it unlikely that the contact experiences will create anxiety or resentment. Second, the management decision-maker may exaggerate the intensity of white worker reaction to Negro job assignments. If the job fulfills a need for the white worker, economically and/or psychologically, he will repress any expression of his feelings in favor of his continued employment. In studies of minority group employment, one of the most consistent findings is that management decision-makers are inclined to exaggerate the anticipated reactions of white workers and customers, even when a Negro is assigned to a supervisory position.

(3) Traditional patterns of job assignment. Still another impediment to equal opportunities in employment for Negroes is the frequent division of the job hierarchy into white and Negro jobs. Certain jobs become assigned traditionally to Negroes, and, regardless of personal abilities, the Negro is automatically assigned to one of these upon hiring. The reasons for initial assignment may vary, but the process results in departments or other predominantly Negro units. In some instances in the South, this pattern has been reinforced by segregated Negro unions that give public expression to this division of labor. These conditions develop a situation in which newly hired employees are placed in jobs that clearly do not take into account their potential or capabilities. Thus, a frame of mind or a predisposition exists to place new Negro employees in service jobs or low-level production jobs and to avoid placing them in technical and high-level production jobs.

(4) Reticence of Negro workers to bid for new jobs or training. The stereotypes of Negro capacities, combined with traditional

patterns of Negro job placement, have both a psychological and a vocational impact on the Negro worker. Psychologically, the existence of such barriers may be translated into apathy toward the job and pessimism about chances for advancement or training. In cases where advancement is tied to bidding for jobs or for training opportunities, the Negro worker may be reticent about such outward shows of ambition or attitudes toward achievement, preferring not to "rock the boat." He may also anticipate that such moves will be rebuffed and will possibly impair his present position in the company. There may also be anticipation that, if he is successful, he will face an environment of hostile co-workers or supervisors who will not support him in his new position. Of equal importance is the fact that these traditional attitudes toward Negro placement may predispose the Negro worker to avoid training opportunities during his job-preparatory years, even if such training is available.

(5) Departmental or supervisory flexibility in job assignments and placements. The conflict between the personnel department and line officers in the placement and assignment of workers is legendary. In initial selection and recommended placement, the personnel office utilizes a series of rational techniques designed to restrict personal biases in the choice of personnel. Frequently, however, the line supervisor is given some flexibility in placement or job assignment, sometimes by choosing from a preferred list of candidates or by retaining a veto over one candidate. This choice is made not only on the basis of competence but also on the potential "fitting-in" of the new worker. The social pressures of a given work situation may well limit the influence of individual competence and overemphasize social and psychological factors. In a department where there is strong group cohesion or a marked similarity in backgrounds among the workers, the supervisor may be hesitant to introduce a Negro for the first time, no matter what his technical qualifications may be. Since the supervisor possesses a certain flexibility of choice in placement or work assignment, the extent to which the Negro is perceived as "different" from the members of his prospective work group may be a significant factor in his initial placement and subsequent job progress.

(6) Informal pressures and hostilities in the work environment. It should not be overlooked that the Negro worker is part of a network of social relationships present in the work place and that the pressures and hostilities of these relationships can influence his job progress. Co-workers can significantly aid or impair the Negro worker's opportunities in the work situation in a number of ways. First, opportunities for promotion or job advancement depend to some extent on informal learning practices. The worker--white or Negro--who is shown the intricacies of technological processes or machine operation by friendly co-workers has significantly advanced his opportunities for promotion, particularly if no formal training program exists. Similarly, the worker who lacks access to such learning finds his opportunities for advancement limited.

Second, bidding for jobs and training opportunities may well depend on two kinds of support given by the work situation--informational and psychological. Access to inside information about the availability of openings and requirements for mastering the job may be as important as seniority in helping the worker to progress. This information is rarely available on a formal basis but exists as part of informal group knowledge open only to workers who are psychologically identified as belonging to the group. Bids for advancement are often encouraged or discouraged depending on the extent of psychological support given or withheld to the potential candidates or the pressures transmitted to the supervisor through informal work groups. The opportunities of the Negro worker must be measured against the friendliness or hostility of his work environment.

(7) Overqualification and underplacement in job assignment. In some cases, the Negro may be required to produce superior credentials in training, education and potential to do the same work assigned to less qualified whites. The phenomenon of the "over-qualified Negro" is most evident in the initial employment of Negroes in a given company, department or unit. The test case Negro worker frequently fills the same role as that held by Jackie Robinson in baseball--he must provide an example of a gifted performer who defies all the stereotypes.

Overqualification, however, introduces several difficulties into equalizing opportunities. The penetration of certain job categories by Negroes is delayed, since it is obvious that the search is on for clearly superior individuals to fill the job. In turn, the Negro's overqualifications may lead the company to set unrealistic standards by which it judges his job performance. Since his credentials are superior, a superior performance is expected, and average, acceptable performance is questioned. His overqualifications for the job may also make him a threat to white workers who have average qualifications. Finally, the Negro worker may resent the fact that, in order to qualify for the job, he must be superior and cannot be judged by the same standards used for the white workers around him. The very existence of a dual qualification system may emphasize to him that he is "different" and, therefore, not "equal."

The Negro may be subjected to underplacement--assignment to a job that is clearly below his qualifications. The reasons for underutilization may be many. First, the company may assign a Negro to a job where he "fits in" harmoniously, regardless of whether his talents are being used. Second, the Negro may be assigned to a job that is "traditionally Negro," with the use of his training and talents a secondary consideration. Third, the company frequently does not recognize technical knowledge that the Negro possesses because it was not acquired through conventional channels. Thus, the Negro who knows electronics may not be placed in an electronics job simply because he acquired this knowledge through correspondence courses rather than in a recognized technical institute. Finally, the company may be unaware of a Negro worker's special talents because they were not revealed in the initial hiring process. All of these conditions may reinforce traditional Negro job patterns.

## PLACEMENT AND EQUAL EMPLOYMENT OPPORTUNITIES

Practices associated with the placement of Negro workers rest both on myth and experience. Reports of our executive respondents on their company's placement procedures varied considerably; experiences and opinions were contradictory in many cases. As in the case of recruitment, there is general agreement that special procedures must be applied in initial placements of Negroes in the company or department in contrast to placements made once a substantial Negro work force exists. For the most part, these special procedures are viewed as temporary measures designed to meet a number of anticipated or real problems.

### Initial Placement Practices

Our executive respondents unanimously agreed that initial placements of Negroes must have the support of the authority and prestige of high-level company officers. It was argued that placement could proceed successfully only if various levels of the company recognized that the employment of Negroes was accepted company policy and would not be modified to meet the objections of any individual or group.

One of the consistent experiences reported by our executive respondents was that few of the anticipated problems related to Negro placements actually occurred. In only a few instances did white workers or customers voice opposition to the placement, and, in these cases, opposition was by individuals rather than by groups and sporadic rather than organized. The treatment of individual cases of worker opposition appears to be fairly uniform--a verbal or written warning that overt acts of opposition would be grounds for dismissal. Only in a small number of cases did a white worker quit his job as a show of opposition to a Negro placement. It appears to be conclusive that, faced with loss or dismissal from a valued job, the white worker overtly curbs his resentment and accepts the situation. It was also apparent that few customers changed their purchasing habits because the company had employed Negroes. In one rare case of organized opposition, the white workers in a southern plant engaged in a letter-writing campaign to customers of the company's fertilizer plant in another community, urging an economic boycott of company products. The campaign lasted for six months but apparently had only a small impact on sales. It is certainly significant that the workers did not promote organized opposition in the plant of their own employment.

One of the problems frequently anticipated by companies in the initial hiring of Negroes is organized community opposition, particularly in the South. This may take the form of increased taxes and decreased community services for the company. Such fears are not well founded and overlook the nature of interregional competition for industry. Nor does it appear common, judging from the evidence of this study, for organized community opposition to develop from civic or fraternal associations. In one case, a bowling alley refused to permit a company's integrated bowling teams. The company moved its bowling activity to a bowling alley on the outskirts of the city. After a three-month period, the owner of the first establishment relented and invited the company's integrated teams to use his establishment. The experiences of the executive respondents in this study indicate that opposition is sporadic and disappears in the face of company determination. The two working principles frequently cited were: Be firm, and be consistent.

The consequences of inconsistency and lack of firmness in initial placements can be seen in the experiences of a southern manufacturing plant. Six female Negro employees were hired in a previously all-white department of fifty-six machine operators. Supervision in the department had been weak and nominal for some time, and the workers enjoyed a rare degree of autonomy. When the Negro workers were introduced--without any preparation of the white workers--a number of the older workers voiced serious objections. The absentee rate doubled; production dropped. A committee of white workers visited the plant superintendent and requested the dismissal of the Negro workers. The management finally agreed to their demand, but only after a series of concessions to the white workers had failed to reduce the opposition. It was apparent that the lack of firmness on the part of the supervisors in making concessions was a factor increasing the opposition activity of the whites. The initial posture of the managerial and supervisory employees toward the placement becomes a reference point for opposition or acquiescence.

Although all of the respondents agreed that the first Negro placement should not be chosen at random, there were many opinions, often contradictory, about the characteristics of the ideal first placement. The following response patterns were evident in the interviews with our management respondents:

(1) The first Negro should have above average qualifications for the job. Since the performance of the first Negro employee will be watched carefully, he should possess superior qualifications to offset stereotypes about Negro work performance. Considerable

care has been taken by most companies to screen the qualifications of the first Negro hirees; overqualification has been the general result. Several of the respondents noted, however, that overqualification in placement may offer certain dangers. The first Negro employee may perform so far above average that he may antagonize white workers who have lower performance profiles and create an expectation that Negroes are "rate-busters" in employment situations. Overperformance may also develop another stereotype of the overproductive Negro worker, making it difficult for subsequently hired Negro workers to satisfy the expectations of supervisors and co-workers. A plant manager in the Midwest noted that he had more success with initially hired Negro workers who were average performers and, therefore, more representative of the Negroes later employed. He felt that overqualified initial placements created a morale problem both for the Negro workers and white co-workers. The Negro worker may particularly resent the need to overqualify and overperform, since this sets him apart from the average workers in the plant.

(2) The job should be visible, functional and open-ended in promotion potential. The emphasis on visibility was particularly strong. It serves two purposes. First, the white workers are made to recognize that Negro employment is an accepted fact and not merely in the planning stages. Second, such placements indicate a symbolic commitment to integrated employment, which customers and community members can view. The vice-president of a small Midwest electronics company reported that there is often a danger that job visibility may become an end in itself (i.e., tokenism). Initial placement practice in his company emphasizes jobs which are "normally," rather than artificially, visible. The first placements in his company were in messenger service and machine maintenance. Both of these jobs necessitate extensive personal contact with a wide range of work stations and company personnel, thus making visibility of Negroes a normal part of the employment situation. It was apparent, however, that, in a number of cases, companies have artificially created high-visibility jobs. In two companies, new jobs have been developed that did not exist prior to the employment of Negroes; in the first, receptionist aides, and in the second, information guides. It is apparent that such jobs were largely token and were developed to avoid the employment of Negroes in the normal job structure.

As a group, the management respondents rejected the concept of nonfunctional employment for Negroes--jobs added to the employment structure that have little value in the company's division of labor but are opportunities to employ Negroes. Although there was considerable agreement that the job should have sufficient prestige and value to be considered desirable, opinions were divided on the desirability of initially placing Negroes in break-in jobs or in employment in the upper levels of the company unit. Proponents of the view that initial placement should be in break-in, or beginning, jobs argue that such placements are more realistic in terms of a company's employment practices and exert minimal pressures on the Negro worker for performance. It is argued that a job at the top of the ladder arouses white worker resentment since deserving white workers may have to be bypassed in making the Negro placement. A beginner's job permits the exposure of a Negro worker to a mobility pattern that requires increasing skill and responsibility for success, obviating the charge that he holds a job for which he has no background. On the other hand, proponents of the view that initial placements should be near the top of the job ladder argue that such placements show the company's commitment to utilize Negro workers and demonstrate the Negro's ability to retain high-level, responsible jobs. Our interviews do not yield sufficient evidence to justify either of these views to the exclusion of the other.

(3) There was strong consensus that the personality characteristics of the first Negro employee were important data to be considered. The initiate should be young, flexible in his dealings with other people and strongly motivated by the job opportunity offered. Considerable emphasis was also placed on the background of the initial placement; he should have had previous contact with whites in a school or work situation and share many of the athletic and aesthetic interests of the white workers. Our interviews show that in the over-all portrait of characteristics, most managers seek Negro workers who have many of the desired emotional, educational and motivational patterns sought in white workers, a natural response in view of the experience with a wholly white work force.

The select portrait of personal characteristics for the first Negro employee obviously impede the recruitment and placement of suitable Negro candidates. The response patterns of our executive respondents suggest that the selection standards for technical ability and personality characteristics of the first men in are, indeed, more demanding than those used for comparable placements of whites. The difficulty in meeting these standards, combined with the inherent discriminatory features of employment testing, act to extend the disadvantage of Negroes in the labor market.

(4) The respondents also suggested that the structure of the department chosen for the initial placement must be selected with care. Two rules-of-thumb were frequently cited. First, the department should be characterized by high mobility to provide the Negro with a chance for promotion. Departments where few promotions are possible are to be avoided because of the consequent competition among workers.

A number of respondents felt that employing the initiate on a trial basis reduces opposition; his white co-workers do not perceive him as a permanent job threat. After the Negro worker is accepted, he can be reassigned to permanent status.   The notion of a "trial-basis placement" was criticized by a southern plant manager. He felt that assignments on a temporary basis invited organized pressures from whites to make the trial period look bad. The experience in his company indicated that white workers accepted initial Negro placements when these were perceived to be permanent and irreversible.

(5) Care must also be exercised in the selection of a supervisor for the initially hired Negro worker. Reports from the executive respondents in our study yield the following composite picture: The supervisor must be a person who has had successful experiences in handling interpersonal relations in his work group; he should have a high prestige standing in his work groups; ideally, he should have moderately high work standards for his department and be strongly motivated to meet these standards. The argument is that a supervisor with high work standards will attempt to integrate the Negro into a functioning role in his department and subordinate worker behavior (e.g., discrimination) that might threaten these standards.

Some companies had success in using older supervisors with a long period of service with the company, whereas younger supervisors were preferred in other companies. The proponents of the younger supervisor group believed that younger executives were less tied to traditional company practices and were more likely to accept new Negro employees because of their contact with Negroes in school or in the Armed Services. On the other hand, older supervisors tended to have higher prestige and could undoubtedly be effective if they were willing to commit their support to the company's equal employment opportunity program.

The attitudes and motivation of the supervisor were considered to be an important factor in both initial and subsequent placements. Although much of the evidence is anecdotal, there appear to be important "do's and don'ts" of supervision that can affect the outcome of initial placements. First, the supervisor should, in some manner, discuss the placement with his workers, emphasizing that company policy in support of Negro employees will be firmly applied. It is apparent that, at the beginning, there is considerable testing of the company's commitment to the placement; the supervisor's pronouncements are the immediate reference points through which white workers can test the company's firmness of intent. Second, the supervisor introduces the Negro worker into the group and, at that time, should make clear the nature of his work and his exact work duties. More sensitive supervisors frequently spend a major portion of the first day personally explaining the nature of the job, lunching with the initiate and personally introducing him to key workers. In some cases, this informal orientation may include the supervisor's superior, although, as a general rule, the tendency is to leave the introduction in the hands of the departmental or unit head. This supportive period should be brief, and, as soon as possible, the supervisor should move toward normalizing the relationship of the initiate to the other workers. A protracted period of protection, it was reported, produces a negative reaction from white workers as well as the new Negro employee; such a situation is artificial and sets the initiate off from the other workers. There are apparently no specific guidelines for the selection of a supervisor; successful supervision will vary from situation to situation depending on interpersonal conditions within a department.

(6) Whether there should be special preparation or orientation of Negro workers before work integration is a debated question. Apparently, there are arguments for and against these strategies. Respondents who argued against special preparation of the Negro felt that such attempts communicate to the Negro that he is different, thus raising his anxiety. It may also make him the object of white worker resentments because he is receiving favored treatment. Those who favored special preparation emphasized that the Negro's anxiety might be allayed by a frank discussion of the problems that he might face as well as the potential trouble spots and how he might best deal with them. Only four of the twenty companies in this study did have formal orientation programs for Negro workers, but an additional ten companies reported that an informal orientation program was operative, leaving considerable flexibility in the hands of local plant personnel officers. In companies with informal orientation programs, the type and length of orientation differed depending on the perceived maturity of the Negro job-holder and the company's assessment of possible white worker resistance. The evidence that could be cited in favor of a formal or informal orientation program or the absence of any program is scant; few companies have an evaluation scheme to determine the relative effectiveness of any of these approaches. A large West Coast aerospace company did some evaluation of orientation vs. non-orientation of new Negro hirees as an element in subsequent adjustment on the job. The limited findings of this evaluation seems to indicate that orientation of Negro workers, individually before hiring, reduced many of their anxieties and significantly affected their work experiences after employment. This same company's experience with orientation programs indicated that in some cases there should be a follow-up series of contacts with the Negro worker during the first six months of employment. The official from this company stressed, however, that such follow-ups were not the rule for all Negro workers but were only for those who responded positively to the opportunity or those judged to need such follow-up counseling.

(7) A collateral question is whether white workers should be given any special preparation or orientation prior to the hiring of the first Negro employee. Again, there is considerable disagreement. While there is widespread agreement on firmness of application, twelve of our executive respondents felt that special preparation of whites could generate a sensitivity to the "special event" of Negro

employment. These respondents reported that there was no special announcement of initial Negro employment to white workers, nor was there any attempt to prepare them for it. Even in these cases, however, special emphasis was placed on the dissemination in company newspapers and on bulletin boards of the company's general policy on minority group employment.

Two companies in this study had special orientation programs for white workers programs which combined formal and informal procedures. It was clear that, in both cases, the intent of the orientation was twofold: to acquaint the workers with company policy on equal employment opportunity and to ascertain which employees might offer resistance. In both cases, the primary method was through meetings of supervisors during which the information was communicated and the resistance diagnosed. It was also a favored practice to follow up this meeting with personal warnings to workers who expressed resentment against Negro employment. As part of their general orientation on joining the company, new white employees were informed of the company's racial employment policy. Both managers in these firms emphasized that orientation of white workers should not be structured as an attempt to win popular approval for the employment of Negroes. The orientation should stress the commitment of the company to the move, its firmness in application of the policy and the requirement that all workers comply with the policy. The orientation session in the two instances above was an opportunity to transmit and clarify information, rather than an open discussion of the pros and cons of the policy. As in the case of Negro orientation programs, there have been no attempts to evaluate the efficacy of these orientations for white workers.

### Regular Placement Practices

To what extent do initial placement practices persist? In other words, do initial placement practices continue as more Negroes enter company employment, or is there a movement away from special practices toward normal employment procedures? Thirteen of the twenty company executives felt that initial placement procedures were temporary, designed to bridge a period of uncertainty, and could be discontinued after the first Negroes entered employment. Seven of the respondents felt that special placement procedures must persist in Negro employment.

It seems clear from our executive interviews that modification of initial employment practices does occur with increase in Negro employment. Recruitment of Negroes and assessment techniques tend to move in the direction of "normal" practices for the work force. The same is partly true of placement. After hiring an initial core of Negro employees, the company moves toward the ideal of hiring all qualified Negroes who apply for job openings. In practice, however, there is still evidence of special exceptions in procedures made for the placement of Negroes. This generally takes five forms. First, some companies have adopted the "scatter technique." As new Negroes are hired, regardless of their particular employment requests, there is a tendency to place them in a department where no Negroes are employed in order to "open it up." As a result, even when the Negro work force is sizable, there may still be special needs for Negro pioneers, requiring special placement procedures. Second, some companies favor the buddy system, in which two or more Negroes are placed in a department. If, through job attrition, the desired number of Negroes in a department declines, there is a tendency to place a Negro in that department when a new Negro worker is hired. Third, once a Negro is placed in a high-level job, there is a desire to avoid "reselling" the job (i.e., repersuading corporate decision-makers that a Negro can succeed in that job). Such a position may have a "Reserved for Negroes" sign implicitly appended to the job, and new Negro hirees may be pointed toward that job. Fourth, the belief may persist in the minds of corporate decision-makers that certain jobs require Negroes with special talents not required of white job applicants. Thus, Negro additions to the sales force of a large appliance company in the Midwest were assigned to predominantly Negroes sales areas. The executive respondent felt that a Negro would speak the same language as his customers and that it would take a Negro with a history of extensive contact with whites to do a comparable job in the white community. Finally, some jobs remain open because they are closely identified with Negro workers, while others remain closed because few Negroes have been employed in these positions. In a large electronics firm, the superintendents of the company cafeteria were all female Negro college graduates, but the reference library, although female, did not have a single Negro. In both positions, the requirements were the same--an undergraduate degree. Only one of the cafeteria superintendents had a background in home economics; the others had backgrounds in history, biology, English literature, library science and sociology. The executive respondent noted that this condition existed because it had been felt in the past that the large number of Negro cafeteria workers would prefer Negro rather than white supervisors. There is no doubt that these five forms will continue to introduce deviations in placements for well-qualified Negroes.

## Factors Influencing Negro Placement

Under what conditions are Negroes considered for a wider range of jobs in a company? We can specify seven sets of influences that shaped placement opportunities for Negro employees in the companies studied: economic; community; technology; "great man" decision; legislation; pressures from civil rights organizations; and organized pressure by Negro workers. Let us consider each one of these in turn:

(1) Economic. There is no doubt that a major influence has been economic necessity. As skill shortages developed in certain occupational categories, intensive searches were undertaken to fill these positions. In some cases, these positions could be filled by underutilized Negroes engaged in less skilled work in the company; therefore, an intensive review was made of the training and skills of Negroes already employed in the company. A second source of scarce manpower skills consisted of the many Negroes who had acquired specialized training in the Armed Forces, in civil service employment and in private Negro companies. Finally, the southern Negro colleges offered an untapped reservoir of skilled Negro manpower. As reported by our executive respondents, all of these "new" sources of skilled manpower made significant alterations in the Negro placement pattern. Just as World War II was the first major influence shaping Negro placement patterns, the manpower shortages of the 1950's made new inroads.

Two other economic trends added to the pressures favoring placement of Negroes. The first was the relocation of certain industries from areas of low Negro population to areas of high Negro population, particularly in the South. A large electronics firm located entirely in a Midwest state relocated 55 percent of its facilities to other regions between 1950 and 1958. A food-processing company has opened three new plants in the southern states. A second pressure was the extensive development of new plants in all areas of the United States. Since these plants started without a tradition of segregated employment, little thought was given to restricted patterns of Negro placement. In the field work, it was obvious that equal employment opportunities in placement--as well as recruitment, assessment, promotion and training--were maximal in new plants and considerably less in older establishments. This observation would argue that traditional patterns of manpower utilization in themselves become the basis for Negro exclusion from equality of opportunity.

(2) Community. It is quite clear from observations in this study that the community context in which work integration occurs can be a strong influence in shaping placement patterns. Without exception, communities where considerable biracial mixing had already occurred (schooling, housing, shopping) tended to have plants with placement patterns more favorable to the Negro. It was also the case that companies located in communities with a large number of integrated plants were more likely than others to present a favorable placement pattern of Negro employment. Finally, the firms located in communities where biracial employment based on talent and skill levels was already an established or growing practice had placement profiles more favorable to the Negro than did others. These observations suggest that the placement profiles of firms located in northern communities were more favorable than those of southern-based firms, and this was indeed the case in the plants studied.

Two other community factors loom large. In several of these communities, there appeared to be a community "pacesetter" in equal employment practices. This company acted as an industry pattern-setter in collective bargaining. Policies and practices developed within the company were quickly established in other firms in the community. The executives of the pacesetter appear to exert an inordinate influence in the development of new recruiting practices and new placement patterns. There does not appear to be a common denominator to the four pacesetters noted in this study. Each one of the plants, however, had been established for a long period of time in its respective community, was a unit of a national company with substantial assets and had contributed to the employment possibilities of a considerable portion of the working force in the community.

There were substantial differences in community training facilities available to Negro youth. In two of the companies located in large midwestern cities, the placement profiles of Negro workers were characterized by proportionately high employment in white-collar and technical jobs. The recruiting officers of these companies indicated that they placed specific job orders at a number of vocational and clerical schools with substantial Negro enrollment. In another company, several skilled worker jobs had been filled by Negroes who were recruited from a community-sponsored pre-apprenticeship school. At the other extreme, the placement profiles of Negro workers were generally poor in communities where Negro high school curricula emphasized service industry skills (home-making, domestic service) and lacked modern facilities in mechanical arts training.

(3) Technology. Our interviews with executives also indicated that technological change can play an important role in shaping Negro placement patterns. The vice-president of a steel company in the Midwest felt that technology in his company affected Negro placements in three ways. First, not every worker eligible by seniority had the basic skills for the operation of the new grinding machines introduced into a department. This permitted placement into the machine job on a nonseniority basis. A number of Negroes benefited from this practice. Second, high-seniority workers frequently desire to remain at their old jobs rather than bid for openings in newly created departments, a situation which favored low-seniority of newly-hired Negroes. Finally, some of the older machine jobs are left vacant when a high-seniority worker bids into another job. Frequently, these machine jobs are not regarded as secure employment because the job that is performed can be eliminated or combined in some other process. For the Negro, such jobs may offer a rare opportunity to move into a machine job, in itself a step upward from unskilled or service employment.

In eight of the manufacturing firms in this study, the bulk of expanded Negro employment occurred in the semiskilled machine jobs. To some extent, this gain is not at the expense of whites, who are increasingly moving into white-collar employment. To the extent that technology is increasing white-collar jobs for whites, the resulting shortage of workers for blue-collar jobs favors the placement of Negroes into the semiskilled ranks of blue-collar work. Although this means blue-collar employment for Negroes who might otherwise have been restricted to unskilled or service employment, it does not result in the placement of Negroes into jobs that have a built-in stability since it is the lower-level blue-collar jobs that are most subject to unemployment and layoff.

(4) "Great man" decision. Significant changes in placement activities may occur by the action of one or more influential individuals within a company. The decision itself may be based on moral grounds or on belief in equalizing opportunities. Fifteen of our executive respondents credited changes in placement policies to the forceful decision of one or more significant individuals in the company. In a large steel company in the Midwest, it was reported that an executive officer of the company had forcefully argued for the placement of some Negro workers in nonfoundry jobs shortly before the Korean War. In spite of the fact that there were considerable threats and opposition from a number of white workers, the officer's views persisted. The exact dynamics of how such individuals translate these decisions into practice was not known in any of the cases reported, but apparently the "great man" decision can shape placement practices.

(5) Legislation. It was also apparent that the actions of federal compliance officers and investigators from fair employment practices commissions influenced the placement profile, although the evidence indicates that the major impact of such agencies was to increase the size of Negro employment rather than to open new jobs for placement. The limited data of this study indicate that in three of the companies protracted pressure from federal compliance and state agency officials resulted in the placement of Negroes into skilled trade jobs, although union membership was withheld from them at the onset. In a large electronics company, repeated complaints from federal compliance officers resulted in the opening of white-collar jobs to Negro women. Although it is difficult to isolate the relative effect of these pressures on placement, it seems likely that such activities do result in some opening of nontraditional jobs, and the significance of these activities may be less in the number of Negroes affected than in the development of new placement patterns.

(6) Civil rights organizations. The activities of civil rights organizations can influence Negro placement patterns in at least two ways. First, the selective use of boycotting or picketing may result in regular conferences between the target company and civil rights officials to modify Negro placement patterns. In one instance, a retail food chain agreed to hire Negro produce countermen and cashiers, two positions that had previously been closed

to Negroes. In the same chain, another picketing incident resulted in the hiring of a Negro bookkeeper. Second, some Negro civil rights organizations attempt to work cooperatively with the personnel officer of some companies to fill specific jobs with Negroes. Six of the companies in our sample had turned to the Urban League to recruit Negroes for specific openings, and these jobs represented new placement patterns.

(7) Organized pressure by Negro workers. Some new patterns of job placement have emerged from the efforts of Negro workers who are underutilized in the company or who are aware of job openings that are closed to them. In an electronics plant in the South, the Negro workers in a local industrial union threatened to bring court action against the union and complained to the international officers when it became apparent that certain categories of jobs were closed to them. After lengthy negotiations, some slight modification in the placement pattern resulted when three Negro employees were placed in the line of progression for jobs previously closed to Negroes. In a large steel mill in the Midwest, Negro foundry workers exerted considerable pressure to open nonfoundry jobs to Negro workers. These efforts became successful when the Negro membership gained sufficient political power to influence the election of officers.

## Negro Job Placement Programs

In the present study, there was a relative lack of experimentation and/or innovation with new patterns of Negro placement. While there have been some remarkable single instances of new Negro placements (e.g., sales), there has been no large-scale movement of Negroes into jobs that have traditionally been barred to them. The failure to place large numbers of Negro workers in traditionally non-Negro jobs is explained in the following arguments given by our management executives:

(1) There are few Negroes who have the adequate preparation for these jobs. An oft-cited expression is, "Bring a qualified Negro to us, and we will hire him." Few attempts have been made to place the marginal Negro applicant in these jobs and supplement his job experience with special training to develop his potential. Such experimentation has been made with some success in lower-level clerical jobs for Negro women. In one manufacturing company, eight Negro women were interviewed for secretarial employment but apparently lacked the necessary skills. On the urging of the company personnel manager, the women were hired for jobs immediately subordinate to secretarial employment. They were encouraged to use company equipment to upgrade their skills for secretarial work. Six of the women eventually moved into secretarial positions. In recounting this story, the personnel officer admitted that this was

not "normal" practice in the company, but reflected a strong desire to integrate the office work force. The expectation among the majority of executive respondents was that the necessary skills for a job should be acquired <u>before</u> employment and certainly not at company expense.

(2) <u>Some Negroes may have the adequate technical preparation but lack necessary social skills needed in the job.</u> The major thrust of this argument is that Negroes come from a "different" cultural background and do not possess the verbal cues of white middle-class people. Therefore, this "culture gap" will interfere with the job performance of the Negro, especially if the job involves extensive contact with whites. The validity of this argument is open to some doubt since there has been no attempt to examine this "culture gap" hypothesis in mass job performance data.

(3) <u>Many Negroes do not have sufficient extra-work contacts with whites and thus lack an understanding of white behavior and motives.</u> This argument is frequently cited to defend the absence of Negroes in the company sales force. Combined with (2), the implication is that Negroes have a culture of their own, unintelligible to whites, and at the same time find white middle-class culture unintelligible.

## Jobs Without Negroes

In concluding our discussion of placement, it might be well to consider the characteristics of jobs that appear resistant to Negro employment. We can specify five major characteristics of the many job areas that had few Negroes in our study:

(1) <u>The jobs most resistant to Negro employment are those that require close, personal contacts with whites in the sale of an article that is competitively available on the market.</u> This includes most high-level selling jobs.[1] For the most part, Negro salespeople operate in Negro neighborhoods or with Negro clientele. In one significant instance, an industrial manufacturing company reported the use of Negro salespeople, but the product involved was not generally available on the market. It was widely reported by our management respondents that few Negroes applied for these sales jobs, and, if they did, they requested assignments in or near a big city, thus severely restricting their mobility.

---

[1] A significant exception is the use of Negro salesladies in retail trade. In the retail chain studied for this report, however, the greatest number of Negro salesladies were in retail stores with a large Negro clientele.

Three reasons are frequently cited for failure to employ more Negroes in sales positions: fear of customer reaction; anxiety about the effect on white salesmen; and fear that the Negro will not be able to carry on social participation with prospective white customers outside the office. In the limited number of cases available in this study, there was evidence that some of these fears are justified in some instances and not in others. Systematic data do not exist to permit an assessment of performance of Negro salespeople at this time.

(2) Jobs in the direct line of progression for an executive or administrative position make up a second job group resistant to Negro employment. Male Negro workers have been employed in the office of a large manufacturing plant, but outside of the line of progression that leads to supervisory or office manager positions. A large electronics company employed a number of Negro engineers who were involved in technical functions rather than administrative assignments that lead to an executive position. In a retail food chain, Negro women have been hired into cashiers' jobs but not into jobs that might lead to a section managership.

(3) The third group of jobs resistant to Negro employment is the higher-level secretarial jobs that are integral parts of the inner structure of management. Although fifteen of the companies in this study had at least one Negro secretary, these jobs tended to be considerably below the top secretarial positions in the office. Three reasons were given for the absence of Negro females in these jobs: the jobs involve more experience than any Negro applicant has had thus far; the jobs involve contact with people outside of the company and might cause resentment; and the jobs involve extensive contact with white secretaries in the same jobs, and conflicts might arise.

(4) The last group of jobs that resist Negro penetration are those jobs that permit the job-holder sufficient seniority to bid for jobs in other offices in a different geographical area. These jobs present the possibility that a Negro could bid into a job in an all-white district or into an office where he might be resented. The only evidence on transfers by bidding is in a retail food chain in the Midwest. The vice-president reported that, of twelve Negroes given the chance to bid on jobs in white areas, all declined, expressing a preference for employment closer to their homes, usually in all-Negro neighborhoods. This very limited evidence suggests that, given the chance, Negroes resist being "pioneers" and do not bid for jobs in an apparently hostile environment.

## TRAINING AND EQUAL EMPLOYMENT OPPORTUNITIES

The role of training in the development of equal employment opportunities has been one of paramount importance. Among our executive respondents, there was almost complete agreement that, relative to white entrants, Negro entrants to the labor market lack adequate preparation for work. As we have indicated previously, the problem is threefold. First, the school dropout rate among Negro youth is three times that of white youth, and, although the rate has been dropping, the relative advantage of white youth is still apparent. Second, even when Negro youth complete high school, the quality of a high school education in a segregated or inner-city school may be inferior to the educational preparation given to whites. Thus, even with a high school diploma, the Negro youth is frequently at a disadvantage in the labor market. Finally, vocational education, even when it does exist in the ghetto school, lacks the sophisticated, up-to-date mechanical equipment of the vocational school in the white neighborhood. Frequently, the curriculum in vocational education in Negro schools reflects the narrow range of jobs--service or manual--that are regarded as Negro jobs. These flaws in child and youth education frequently translate themselves into a psychological state of pessimism, hostility and anxiety about the acquisition of training for the labor market.

### Company Training Programs

The first observation about company training programs is that most companies do not have institutional training programs. Most training in American industry is informal, on-the-job training, heavily dependent on the supervisory efforts of the foreman or department head and the cooperative aid supplied by long-service co-workers.

Besides institutional and on-the-job training, there are two other training forms frequently found in American industry: tuition grant and apprentice training. In the first, the student attends classes at some outside training installation, and the company pays his tuition. In apprentice training--usually associated with skilled craft preparation--the union establishes standards and makes provision for training, using its own or outside educational facilities. The company may also conduct special instruction classes to fill particular skill needs as they arise. A large business machine concern conducted a six-week course of instruction in new business methods for old as well as new employees. A midwestern steel mill organized a fifteen-week course in pre-apprenticeship training for apprentice candidates who lacked specific mathematical skills to qualify for apprentice training.

There are two points at which training has considerable significance for the Negro worker: compensatory training to eliminate past disadvantages and training opportunities that bridge the knowledge gap between jobs and lead to promotions.

Although several exceptions were to be noted, few of the training structures of the companies studied afforded compensatory or supplementary vocational training. The general pattern was to support and partially subsidize these forms of training in agencies external to the company. However, even when this support appeared, the tendency was to fund a specific program for a short period of time. In several instances, there was cooperative funding by a number of companies. A basic literacy program for prevocational training was funded by six companies in a northeastern city. Forty prospective employees attended, but only seven received any employment from the sponsoring companies in the six months following training. Our executive respondents clearly believed that compensatory education could best be handled by agencies outside of the company.

It appears clear that the companies in this study made limited use of federally financed or community-financed programs of prevocational training to fill existing manpower needs or to further Negro employment. Only two of the firms studied reported that they made use of on-the-job training subsidies to improve the skills of Negro workers. Most of the executive respondents lacked knowledge about federally financed training programs and, in general, were suspicious of them. Few of the respondents had extensive contacts with program graduates and possessed little information on the number and resources of such programs.

Three observations about management views of federal training programs seem clear. First, there was a frequent suggestion that students in such programs were "bad boys," "wise guys" or "problem cases," i.e., poor work risks. Second, the majority of the respondents had the notion that inferior standards of training would be substituted for company standards if on-the-job training subsidies were used. Finally, management respondents viewed the Negro high school and private training facility as more productive of possible Negro recruits than federal training programs. One exception to these views was expressed by the vice-president of an electronics company who was actively involved in the planning of Manpower Development Training Act (MDTA) training programs. As a general rule, the greater the unfamiliarity or lack of involvement with government programs, the greater the rejection of them.

## The Selection of Negroes for Training

Relatively few Negroes were reported to be in large formal training programs. Our executive respondents were not sure of exact numbers but felt that Negroes participated equally with whites in informal, on-the-job training programs, a belief contradicted by many of our Negro respondents in their interviews. Except in companies in which the union seniority system plays a paramount role in training opportunities, the selection of a worker for training is based on the personal recommendation of his supervisor. In most cases, then, the Negro's immediate supervisor assumes a gatekeeper role regarding his admission to training.

The majority of our executive respondents recognized the possibility of supervisor bias in training selection, but only four of the companies had established procedures to guard against this bias. A large utility in the Midwest conducts an independent check of personnel records on a regular basis to see if Negroes who have the necessary experience are being referred for training. The supervisor is required to justify in writing any failure to refer qualified Negroes. In the other three cases, the checking procedures were less formalized, but spot checks were conducted to see if qualified Negroes were being referred. As part of its supervisor training program, a large electronics company included intensive instruction in equal employment opportunity guidelines to preclude bias in the referral of minority group workers. Our executive respondents agreed that educational efforts by the company to insure that qualified Negro workers were referred for training programs were more effective as a deterrent to biased judgment than procedures to audit the judgments of the supervisor.

Our executive interviews indicated that there were six main pitfalls to be recognized in supervisor referrals of Negroes for training:

(1) Supervisors, especially older ones, may be inclined to see Negroes in certain traditional jobs and, thus, may avoid referring them for training for jobs where Negroes have not been employed.

(2) Supervisors may anticipate a negative reaction from white workers in their departments and avoid referring a Negro for training.

(3) Supervisors may feel that although the Negro is qualified for training, he cannot succeed because of the pressures that will be exerted by white co-workers in the training situation.

(4) Supervisors may consciously or unconsciously use a double standard in referrals, believing that only superior Negroes could

succeed in the training situation, while they refer whites with average performance.

(5) Supervisors frequently review job performance informally and on a personal basis, relying on the informal judgments of other workers as a guide. Since they are unlikely to enjoy close, personal contacts with Negro workers outside of the plant, a negative recommendation from co-workers may work against the Negro's chances for retraining.

(6) Supervisors may uncritically recommend Negro workers for training because they might charge the company with discrimination if they are bypassed.

These pitfalls were more likely to be found in large companies where formal training programs exist. In small companies where on-the-job and informal training programs are the rule, Negroes are dependent for training opportunities on cooperation from long-service workers and the supportive interest of supervisors. Although the majority of our executive respondents admitted that inequality in training opportunities was more likely in such a situation, they felt that, in their own companies, bias in informal training was a minimal problem.

### Willingness of Negroes To Train

A common observation made by our management respondents was that many Negroes did not avail themselves of training opportunities in a formal or informal program, even when special measures were taken to seek out Negroes and encourage them to undertake training. Three reasons were frequently given by our management respondents for this unwillingness to seek training. First, Negroes as a group are less adequately prepared than whites in the pre-employment period and may feel that the competition in the training situation is too much for them. It was a common observation in executive interviews that Negroes lacked self-confidence and initiative and performed below capacity to avoid the possibility of failure. Second, many Negroes, particularly in newly integrated plants, feel that whites will resent their training opportunity and will react with hostility. Third, Negroes frequently have little knowledge or background experience in the new job area, and this lack of information predisposes them to avoid training.[2]

---

[2]Whether this analysis is correct or not must remain an open question, since the causes of Negro unwillingness to train have not been subjected to systematic research.

Four of the companies in this study had developed various practices to overcome an apparent unwillingness of Negroes to undertake training.

A large aerospace company had developed a counseling program for Negroes designed primarily to encourage them to bid for training and promotional opportunities. It is a routine practice to inform Negroes of their eligibility for training opportunities, to discuss the opportunities with them and to encourage them to undertake training. The worker may continue his counseling sessions during training and use the counselor as a resource to discuss and analyze reactions to the training experience. This company has also required that supervisors inform Negroes of possible training opportunities and encourage them to enroll. Unfortunately, the efficacy of counseling in overcoming resistance to training had not been subjected to careful evaluation by this company at the time of the interview.

A prominent electronics company maintains extensive work histories of its workers on electronic tape. Workers eligible for training on the basis of seniority and past job performance are identified and notified. The departmental supervisors are under instructions to work intensively with these eligibles, whites and Negroes, and to enroll them in training. Continued reluctance from the worker results in a scheduled interview with a counselor to review the opportunity and the reasons for refusal.

Although only these two companies operated counseling programs to overcome Negro resistance to training, there was widespread agreement that this would be the most appropriate strategy to use.

### Evaluating the Performance of Negro Workers

The executive respondents in our study were asked to contrast Negro job performance with that of whites. Since training opportunities are largely dependent on past job performance, we assumed that there would be some relationship between these executive evaluations and the extent to which Negroes were encouraged to participate in the training programs. Variations in response patterns were very small. The following conclusions seem justified by these response patterns:

(1) At the lower-level jobs, Negroes were frequently said to be less dependable than white workers. Some executives clarified their remarks by indicating personal characteristics which are barriers to training: poor personal appearance; lack of grooming; lack of sophistication in presenting themselves to co-workers and employer; and a "chip on the shoulder" attitude. Garnishment of wages was viewed as a major problem. However, on absenteeism, work discipline and actual performance, these Negroes were considered "average."

(2) Many of these complaints did not apply to Negro workers in skilled or white-collar jobs, in which Negro performance was rated as "average or better." However, a common characterization given of Negro office workers is that, as a group, they are less willing than whites to accept transfers or added responsibilities.

(3) The greatest satisfaction was expressed with Negroes in technical or professional employment. Frequently, their performance was described as "above average," and they were "able to hold their own."

These evaluations of Negro job performance should be viewed with caution. Evaluations, when expressed in aggregate terms, usually mean very little, and the majority of the executive respondents could cite numerous examples that did not fit this aggregate characterization. The interviewer made three observations about these evaluations: they are too sketchy to have any great significance; the majority of the companies had no evaluation data of Negro performance, so that statements were impressionistic rather than factual; and their value may be in the fact that there are variations in the evaluation of Negro employees in different jobs rather than a blanket statement to cover all Negro workers. On the whole, executives generally expressed satisfaction with the job performance of Negroes in their respective companies.

## PROMOTION AND EQUAL EMPLOYMENT OPPORTUNITIES

Much of what has been said about management experiences with racial practices in training applies equally to promotion. In most companies, the immediate supervisor is the gatekeeper to promotions. The supervisor's recommendation, based on evaluation and assessment of job performance, is the main element in promotional opportunities. Of course, company or union seniority is also a consideration but, in most cases, does not outweigh the influence of the supervisor.

### Obstacles to Negro Promotions

Negro promotional opportunities may be beset by a number of obstacles. Some of these obstacles result from past practices, while others are rooted in the present structure and belief system of the company. As indicated in the executive response patterns, five obstacles would seem to be of major importance in thwarting Negro job promotions:

(1) There appears to be a series of assumptions and beliefs about employment that have implications for Negro promotional opportunities. In a number of companies studied, a high school education is required for jobs above entry level. Since Negroes as a group are more likely than others to lack this educational attainment, promotional opportunities are dimmed. In one of the companies, a past practice included the hiring of Negro workers in their early teens for service employment. Since this group was generally without a high school education, few of them were able to advance in the company. Quite recently, an attempt was made to upgrade this group by offering them tuition-free education in night classes at the company. Of 155 workers in this category, 31 are attending the classes out of an initial enrollment of 39. Several executive respondents indicated that recent upgrading of job requirements at their companies undoubtedly affected Negro promotional opportunities adversely.

(2) It is also clear that Negro promotional opportunities are hampered by the effects of past practices of separate lines of promotion. The past restriction of Negro workers to a narrow range of jobs with no opportunities for promotion into non-Negro jobs may have the following effects. First, it severely restricts the experience capabilities of Negro workers, and thus limits their qualifications for jobs outside the Negro line of job progression. Second, it results in the development of assorted stereotypes of Negro employment that may unconsciously persist and continue to restrict the number of promotional opportunities for which the Negro is considered. In some cases, the fact that Negroes have not been employed in certain categories of jobs may be cited as evidence that Negroes lack capabilities for these jobs. Such practices may also be perpetuated in collective bargaining, making it necessary to renegotiate existing contract provisions of seniority and progression if the Negro is to break out of his narrow range of jobs.

(3) Finally, in many cases, dual selection criteria continue to operate in promotions for Negroes, especially in promotions into non-Negro jobs. It seemed to be implicit in several executive interviews that the company must consider a number of factors, not operative in white promotions, when Negroes are considered for promotion into previously all-white jobs. Such factors include the emotional maturity of the Negro, his relationships with white workers, his ability to cope with white worker resentments and his unquestioned ability to handle the job. One respondent noted that his company felt it was important to open up new job areas for Negroes and would bide its time until the right Negro came along to increase the possibility of success.

The companies that indicated that they are making some progress in increasing Negro promotions reported that they are doing more than just saying "the doors of opportunity are open." They are working on a personal basis with supervisors and employees.

Job reviews tend to be flexible and informal, although basic promotional criteria are not abandoned. Supervisors are urged to
encourage Negroes with potential to bid for promotions once they
are eligible. In a few cases, the Negro employee is not given a
chance to say no, but is placed into the new job and given whatever support is necessary to maintain him.

## Company Promotional Practices

Recognizing that promotions for Negroes may pose special
problems, a number of practices have been developed to stimulate
promotions. Many of the practices follow those discussed under
training:   counseling programs to encourage the job applicant
to seek promotions; a review of promotion policies to insure impartiality; and the development of auditing and educational techniques
to reduce the biases of the supervisors.

A large heavy-manufacturing company has pioneered in a practice that is becoming a model for equalizing opportunities in
promotion. First, the company undertook a thorough review of
promotional criteria used by supervisors to isolate intentional or
unintentional discriminatory practices against Negroes. Second,
this was followed by a thorough and comprehensive review of the
abilities and qualifications of the existing work force with the goal
of filling available job openings from this source. A thorough review was undertaken of the personnel records of Negro employees
who had been confined to service and unskilled jobs. Third, a
personal interview was scheduled with each one of the workers to
review experience and qualifications that might not have been
recorded in the personnel records. The personal interview also
collected extensive data on occupational and training interests.
Fourth, new data on the Negro workers were made available to
their supervisors. Finally, an extended follow-up was developed
to check on supervisor and workers to see if the new information
had been acted upon and with what results. In selected cases, the
Negro workers were encouraged through counseling sessions to
bid for promotions and to avail themselves of training opportunities
that could lead to job advancement.

The executives from two other companies indicated that the
personnel records of long-service Negro employees were generally
inadequate per se as a basis for upgrading. Frequently, at the point
of job entry, the applicant presents only the information he considers
necessary for employment in a particular job in the company.
Some Negroes were undoubtedly motivated to omit significant work
experiences in order to avoid an image of ambition and achievement incompatible with the requirements of service and unskilled jobs.
These respondents also noted that information about unusual training experiences was often not mentioned in the initial hiring process.

In one company, a number of Negroes in the maintenance department were discovered to have scarce construction specialties acquired outside the normal channels of apprenticeship. It would seem to be a justified step to review the possibility of such skills and capabilities.

Although a number of respondents mentioned special considerations in facilitating promotions for Negroes, there was widespread agreement that Negro promotions must remain within the rubric of the company employment structure and the guidelines of established promotional criteria. Preferential treatment as a policy to increase Negro promotions was uniformly opposed, as was the lowering of standards for certain jobs. It was obvious that such ideas violated the norms of business efficiency and were therefore rejected.

CHAPTER 4    CORPORATE STRUCTURE
             AND EQUAL EMPLOYMENT
             OPPORTUNITIES


What organizational factors influence the development and structure of equal employment opportunities? To obtain the answer to this question, we sought information on some of the experiences and organizational problems in administering equal employment practices. We were particularly interested in how the organizational structure of the company related to the profile of equal employment practices and the administrative procedures initiated to maintain them.


## THE DEVELOPMENT AND STRUCTURE OF
## EQUAL EMPLOYMENT OPPORTUNITY PROGRAMS


It is apparent from the interviews in this study that at least one principle governs the development, structure and application of equal employment practices within a given firm. More than any other factor, the structure of the organization shapes the program goals, practices and control procedures. By "structure" we mean both the network of assumptions, beliefs and attitudes about employment in the company and the prevailing pattern of administrative practices in employment. These set limits within which opportunities are made available to minority group members (i.e., the minority group employment practices that are adopted will not be radical departures from existing company practices but, rather, will fit into the network of practices that already exists within the organization). Thus, no single blueprint can be developed to guide all companies, and even general principles must be qualified to fit the particular structure of an organization.


Three Company Profiles in Minority Group Employment


The distinctiveness of minority group employment experiences among companies can be illustrated by reference to three companies in our sample. The first is a large utility in a midwestern city; the second is a national food retail chain with stores in all major cities of 20,000 or more; the third is a chain of family-owned department stores located in three of the north central states. In spite of the fact that each one of these companies had publicly pledged a policy of nondiscrimination in employment, the practices of implementing this policy differ and reflect differences in company organization. The following sketches give some indication of the complexities involved in the development and application of an equal employment opportunity policy:

(1) The first company is the largest utility in its state, supplying its produce to almost 90 per cent of the state's residents. There are branch offices in every community of the state, and each branch closely resembles the structure of every other branch. A strong system of centralized control is exercised through a rigorous reporting system moving from the local unit through a regional division and into corporate headquarters organization. A well-developed procedural system includes extensive guidelines to govern the activities of personnel. The company has pioneered in scientific personnel administration with a heavy emphasis on merit employment and an active recruitment unit based in the personnel department. There is a long tradition of expected involvement in community affairs by all personnel above first-level supervision. A number of special activity departments exist, and the chief officer of each of these departments reports directly to the president.

The company undertook to develop a strong equal employment program in the early 1950's, although some Negroes were already employed in unskilled and service jobs as early as 1948. A special department was established under a vice-president to develop equal employment opportunity practices, to monitor the program and to make recommendations directly to the president. The activities of the recruiting unit were expanded to include visits to institutions in the Negro community. The community-involvement program was broadened to require that all supervisory and executive personnel spend some time in active contact with individuals and organizations in Negro communities to recruit job candidates. A salient feature of the program is a reporting system that requires all units of the company to submit three sets of reports on race and employment: how many job vacancies are unfilled and how many have become filled and by whom; how many Negroes have applied for jobs, who received them, who did not (with complete explanation for rejecting the Negro job applicant) and where were they placed; and detailed accounts of contacts with Negro individuals and organizations. These three sets of data are collated and examined for possible discrepancies. The reports are reviewed by regional or corporate headquarters, and suggestions for improvement are made. The equal opportunities program is headed by a vice-president; the operating head is a Negro with an extensive record of service in

Negro action groups. This special department has extensive power to recommend new procedures or practices in any of the sub-units of the organization. Of particular interest is the extent to which the program draws on existing organizational features and practices for its structure. Thus, there is a tradition of special activity programs, community involvement by supervisory and executive personnel, firmness and control from the top and special monitoring of unit activities.

All of these organization features are basic elements of the equal employment opportunity program, making it possible to institute equal employment practices without radical innovations.

The application of these practices met with little resistance from white workers. Since the company innovates considerably in personnel matters, there is a climate of anticipated change in the organization, and personnel are not expected to question new policies or practices. In all personnel practices, there is a tradition of firmness in application that permits no questioning of procedures. The company has taken pains to explain that one dimension of potential promotability is the extent to which policies and practices are administered firmly by supervisors and obeyed without question by subordinates. It is emphasized that equal employment opportunity policies and practices are "normal" personnel matters, requiring the same response as any other.

(2) The second company differs in a number of important respects from the first. Of utmost importance is its decentralized structure. The degree of control by corporate headquarters is minimal, and the important unit of reference is a regional headquarters. But even within each region, there is a series of relatively autonomous divisions. Each division negotiates its own union contract, if the division is unionized; sets its own personnel policies; does its own hiring; and controls its own purchases. There is a close identification with local community practices, perhaps as a result of the fact that store personnel are recruited from the local communities. A number of the stores are franchised; the property for all stores is leased rather than owned by the company. In contrast to the first company, where emphasis is placed on conformity to the rules and regulations of corporate headquarters, the policy in this company is to encourage local initiative in the development of policies and practices. Directives from corporate headquarters are worded in the most general language, leaving the formulation of practice to the local personnel. A striking feature of this company is the norm of entrepreneurship that dominates most local units, in contrast to the more bureaucratic norms of the first organization. In the first company, promotability depends on the facility in applying rules, regulations and directives; in the second company, promotion potential is largely determined by such factors as individual initiative, independence and self-reliance. In the first company, considerable emphasis was placed on team work and

performance within a group; in the second company, more emphasis was placed on independent action and individual judgment.

Although the company had employed Negroes in some of the stores in large urban areas, few of the Negro workers worked full time. All had menial jobs characterized by low promotion prospects and low pay. In 1962, the company publicly announced an equal employment plant. Efforts to coordinate practice through corporate headquarters offered a number of difficulties. Some stores refused to submit a statistical report on their Negro employees to corporate headquarters. Criticism of the program was made by a number of the independently franchised stores. Each regional unit was made responsible for the stores in its area, but no paper statistical system was developed. A number of the regional headquarters sent a representative once every six months to visit the stores and make an informal evaluation. This information was delivered to regional headquarters, but no feedback was made to the stores involved. No special unit was established within corporate, regional or divisional headquarters to develop equal employment policy or practices. In corporate headquarters, a vice-president of personnel was charged with the responsibility for the program, but this was clearly a secondary activity; there was no staff organization to work with him. At the regional unit observed in this study, three persons were assigned on a limited basis to the program; their duties were concentrated more in public relations activities than in policy formulation and review. Two of the three persons viewed their duties as "putting out brushfires"--handling complaints with a racial basis and advising stores on tactics if they were picketed by Negro action groups. The third member, a Negro woman, visited predominantly Negro high schools to stimulate Negro youths' interest in jobs with the company and participated in community activities in equal employment campaigns as a representative of the company. It was clear that she exercised no policy-making authority and that the job was largely a token activity.

(3) The third company differs from the other two in that it has a strong tradition of family ownership. In the early 1960's, this company, under the direct leadership of its president, proceeded to develop an aggressive equal employment opportunity program as an integral part of its over-all employment policy. The president of the company is a forceful personality with strong personal convictions about equal employment for Negroes.

In this company, there are long-standing, strong personal relationships between corporate level executives, including the president, and managers and supervisors in local retail outlets. Although considerable autonomy is necessarily afforded local managers and supervisors in day-by-day operations, considerable emphasis is placed on direction by executive fiat in policy-decision matters. A principal element in the formulation and review of policy is the personality of the president himself. The president and other corporate executives and officers show a decided preference for informal, personal contact with subordinates, rather than paper systems. A major element in the control and review of practices is the personal visit and telephone calls to local outlets by corporate-level executive staff. Within the company, there is a widely accepted norm that promotion depends on successful and facile compliance with the directives of the president and his staff, and aggressiveness in policy application by local managers is regarded as a virtue.

The accomplishments of the equal opportunity program in this company have been reviewed with considerable favor by several Negro action groups, particularly within one large metropolitan area where over half of the stores in the chain are located. The program has been vigorously developed and pursued with the full backing and encouragement of the president. Company headquarters has required a periodic census of Negro workers in the stores and central warehouse operations, and store managers are expected to be able to comment on the job duties of Negro workers and their prospects for promotion. With respect to this last point, the same expectation is true in regard to all employees, but there is clear evidence of a special sensitivity to the achievements and potential of Negro employees.

The president appointed a Negro as a vice-president of the company, a position with considerable authority and responsibility. This individual, working with other executive staff, has undertaken a review of the work experience, skills and education of many older Negro employees to see if some upgrading or reassignment was not possible. Plans for the development of Negro supervisory and managerial personnel were also initiated. Efforts were successful in placing Negro managerial personnel in stores that were in predominantly white neighborhoods, as were attempts to establish special training programs for Negro school dropouts as part of a job experience program. Not only is there a significant number of Negro employees at all levels of company operation, but their levels of job achievement are high.

This company has also been active in equal employment programs in the community. Following the lead of the president, company staff have participated in Negro community affairs and worked with programs of Negro action groups. A company team composed of Negro executives and employees has been active in developing a stay-in-school program for Negro youths. The company is highly regarded by the Negro community, and the number of job applications by Negroes is consistently high.

Several comments can be made about these three company sketches. First, the development of equal employment opportunities cannot be divorced from the structure of the organization, especially its over-all management of administrative matters. The personnel and management traditions of some companies favor the development of equal employment opportunities more than those of others. Second, such a program must incorporate existing features of the organization to become operative. In other words, the program operates not in a vacuum but in a network of policies, practices and relationships that give the organization a unique stamp. Third, it would be difficult indeed to specify one factor basic to the successful development of a program. In the first company, a tradition of bureaucratic responsibility, close supervision of subordinate activities and an investment of resources in monitoring and collating relevant information undoubtedly yielded results. In the third company, these activities were minimal, but a forceful personality-- the president of the company--and a close, tight, but informal pattern of supervision contributed significantly to the development of a successful program. Finally, it is apparent that these differences in organizational structure may be reflected in a range of practices related to the development of equal employment opportunities. For example, involvement in the Negro community by the first and third companies was high, but it was practically nonexistent in the second company, a fact that would undoubtedly influence the future recruitment of Negroes into the company.

## THE ORGANIZATION OF EQUAL EMPLOYMENT OPPORTUNITY PRACTICES

The development of equal employment practices occurs within an organizational context and shows both similarity and variability from organization to organization. The need for equal employment goals or targets is a necessity in any organization, but the content, determination and application of these goals will vary according to organizational structure and traditions. The same may be said for the control systems or the responsibility structure associated with nondiscriminatory practices. Companies have different structures and managerial styles which must be considered by the developer of any equal employment opportunity program.

Our executive respondents were almost unanimous in the opinion that developing sound equal employment practices offered specific problems of staffing, contact with the community and coordination of company resources not encountered in any other company programs. They attributed this to three causes. First, the development and application of practices are subject to monitoring by a wide number of outside groups--the civil rights agency, the local or state fair employment agency and the contract compliance groups associated with the Federal Government. Second, in some companies there is legal accountability to state or federal agencies in the form of written reports and on-site inspections. In these cases, the employment practices of the company must be held up for inspection and corrected or modified upon request. Finally, many outside groups have the ability to deliver serious sanctions against the company through contract cancellation in some cases, or through boycott, picketing or moral persuasion.

The nondiscrimination practices of a company may be developed within a formal structure with a specialized division of labor, an elaborate system of procedures and staff members who have a full-time commitment and expertise in the development and application of this program. Or the practices may be highly informal, with no specialized personnel. The absence or presence of a formal program is not a good guide to the status of equal employment opportunities in a company, since many firms do maintain substantial activity based on informal procedures rooted in common personnel practices.

### The Initial Stage in the Development of Equal Employment Opportunities

For most of the companies, it was during the years of World War II that it became necessary to consider the problems and procedures for dealing with minority group employment. Some companies had small numbers of Negro employees before that time, confined to jobs isolated from close contact with the white work force. Few Negroes were employed in equal-status jobs with whites. The manpower squeeze of the war, coupled with rising Negro aggressiveness in seeking better jobs, combined to add a new dimension and new problems to the employment structure of most of the companies in this study. In this initial stage, "things were done," practices developed and procedures examined--long predating Plans for Progress and other organized, associational programs--the beginning of the search for guidelines to integrate the Negro into American industry. This search was a voluntary effort to develop procedures to meet company manpower need. It was not until the late 1950's and early 1960's that the element of legal compliance was introduced.[1]

An examination of the early practices and administrative procedures of the twenty companies in this study suggest five important guidelines for the employment of Negroes in American industry. These guidelines are derived from a wide range of experiences in these companies and focus on common rather than unique practices in the early days of the equal employment efforts:

--------------------------------------------------

[1]Some defense-linked companies had experienced legal compliance requirements as early as 1939 under the Roosevelt Administration's contract compliance program.

(1) In developing nondiscrimination practices, the full backing of the top officials and the chief officer of the company was sought.

(2) At the earliest possible time, the employment policy was modified to include a clear, concise statement of the company's commitment to nondiscrimination in employment.

(3) Specific procedures were developed to translate nondiscrimination policy into specific operating practices.

(4) The nondiscrimination policy was communicated to all levels of personnel.

(5) The nondiscrimination policy was communicated to community agencies that influenced the flow of manpower into the company: public and private employment agencies; public and private vocational schools; community high schools; and schools of higher learning.

These five practices, as important as they are, are largely passive orientations toward the problem and will not automatically equalize opportunity. As we have implied in our discussion of employer experiences, opportunities are not equalized by fiat but rather by actions that root out and eliminate discriminatory practices, intentional or unintentional. The company that wants to integrate the Negro must understand that the problem involves an orientation to activity on many levels of company and community, and for this a passive orientation toward the problem will not suffice.

Administering Nondiscrimination Practices

Although each company may develop unique practices, there must be some administrative system to guarantee the continuity of these practices. This may involve a formal or informal structure. We turn to a consideration of the administrative network and problems involved in equal employment implementation in the twenty companies. There are five particular aspects of administration that will be considered: time allocation to activities associated with equal employment opportunity practices; the organization and allocation of staff and other resources to equal employment activities; the responsibility structure; the structure of the control or auditing system; and the evaluation of the effectiveness of equal employment practices. Let us consider each one of these in turn:

(1) <u>Time allocation for equal employment activities</u>. It is clear from the observations on the twenty companies in this study that implementing equal employment policies requires effort in a number of activities both in corporate headquarters and in the local plant. The following is a composite inventory of activities that

characterized the companies in this study. Not all of the twenty companies generated effort in each of these activity areas, but each of the companies engaged in one or more of these activities.

Recruiting minority group members (direct application, schools, colleges, newspaper ads, referrals from company employees).

Contact with Negro organizations (public relations or image building, employment solicitation, conferences).

Contact implementation activities in the field (visits to local plants, fighting "brushfire" situations, personal visits or telephone calls to local representative or department head responsible for equal employment activities).

Headquarters control (survey and analysis of field reports, summary of reports, coordination and feedback to line units, formulation of policy, development of practices).

Contact with federal compliance or local fair employment agency.

Review and continuing analysis of nondiscrimination practices (recruiting, hiring, upgrading, grievance-discipline machinery).

General review of policy (policy revision, setting goals).

Contact with other companies (cooperative community action, conferences on bilateral or affirmative action).

Community relations (contact with Negro community, supportive work with programs to improve Negro manpower prospects).

An ideal affirmative action program would require some degree of commitment and effort in each of these activity areas. What differences in effort, if any, were apparent among the twenty companies? What factors account for the differences or similarities? Let us again consider the activity areas.

The recruitment of minority group members was an activity conducted by each one of the companies and undoubtedly received the most emphasis of all equal employment activities, both on the corporate and local unit level. It was clear that management felt this task had the highest priority. Although there was a basic emphasis on numbers, there were variations in the types of personnel sought. Primary emphasis was placed on college graduates with skills that would fit the manpower needs of the company. There appeared to be little emphasis placed on seeking Negroes for token roles in the company, although this was apparent in a few cases. The basic ideal in recruitment was to find Negroes who could help to meet the manpower shortage in the company, but there was general agreement that adequately trained workers were in short supply.

Contact with Negro organizations and community relations received the second highest time commitment in these companies. The equalizing of opportunities was viewed at corporate headquarters as an activity that had public value, and considerable time was devoted to the cultivation of Negro organizations and participation in activities designed to increase the manpower potential of the Negro. On the local plant level, such activities varied. Contact with Negro organizations was considerably less in southern than in northern locations, and community work was more prevalent in companies that had strong philosophical commitments to contributing to the social life of the communities in which their plants were based.

In defense-linked companies, the contact with federal compliance officials received a major priority. These contacts varied, of course, depending on the profile of minority group employment presented to the compliance officers. Headquarters control in these companies assumed equal importance, since the two activities were linked.

There was a scattering of order or priorities among the other activities, and time commitments apparently reflected basic organizational structure as well as preoccupation with different equal employment problems. Whether the practices and policies were reviewed, how often and by whom reflected unique administrative principles in the various companies. For the most part, there was a "fitting in" of equal employment administrative procedures into the general network of administrative procedures in the company.

These observations suggest that the companies focused their energies on the development of recruiting strategies; indeed, it is in this area that the greatest storehouse of knowledge exists. The structures of other activities were partly predictable with a knowledge of organization structure. Thus, a large electronics company with a southern-based firm exercised headquarters control primarily through a series of detailed manuals on administering equal employment practices. The use of manuals for administration in safety and grievance control is well established in this company, and consequently it seemed natural that the manual concept would be extended to equal employment policy.

(2) The organization of staff. In only two of the companies were there separate departments to administer the program; these departments were closely tied to personnel functions in the company. In both cases, the heads of these departments had been trained in personnel and reported to the vice-president in charge of personnel administration. Several points should be noted about the organization of staff to administer equal employment practices:

(a) Equal employment opportunity practices and policies were viewed largely as personnel matters. In twelve companies, the administration of this program was in the personnel department. In four other companies, the administration was shared by the personnel-industrial relations departments. In two others it was in an administrative department.

(b) In both the corporate headquarters and the local units, the administration of equal employment activities was rarely considered a full-time job. In all but two cases, the administrators of equal employment activities were committed to this during only a small fraction of their total working time. The time commitment ranged from one-eighth to one-half time. Even those with full-time equal employment opportunity work assignments were on call for other duties. As a general rule, the actual time committed varied and was greater during certain periods (e.g., special recruiting campaigns or compliance reviews) and less when these activities were not in process.

(c) The level of knowledge and expertise on equal employment practices varied considerably from company to company. As a group, the corporate staff respondents were more knowledgable and sophisticated than local plant personnel, although there were varying degrees of awareness of minority group employment practices and the problems in applying them among the latter. In four of the cases, the local plant respondents had no clear idea of the content of the company policy or prescribed practices although there was a general awareness of company intent in equalizing employment. Three conditions obviously contributed to the expertise of the local plant respondents: the scheduling of regular conferences and seminars at corporate or regional headquarters to orient local plant decision-makers; the presence of intense community equal employment activity, in which local plant personnel participated (e.g., career days for disadvantaged youth); and the nature of the relationship between corporate headquarters and local operations. In the last case, the better-informed local plant respondents were in companies with relatively little autonomy in local operations and decision-making (i.e., most of the local decisions were corporate decisions); or there was extensive paper control and supervision of the equal employment program from corporate headquarters requiring extensive paper and personal communication with the home office; or there was a regularly scheduled review of personnel activities by corporate staff. A large utility in the Midwest has taken considerable care to indicate that promotions for local administrators will be judged by satisfactory performance in all activities in the local operation, including the administrative activities associated with equal employment. This apparently resulted in strong interest in the program by local people. The head of the program in this company indicated that it is important to inform subordinates that administration of equal employment activities is a major and vital activity in the company's operations and ranks in importance with other major activities in the company.

Three other points should be made about staff. First, in a number of the companies, there was at corporate headquarters access to the services of various minority group employment consultants--usually Negro professionals--to supplement existing company expertise. Extensive use was made of Urban League personnel for this purpose. Relatively little use was made by local plant personnel of such outside expertise in local operations. In six of the companies, Negroes who had background experience in civil rights organizations were employed for various phases of the equal employment program (e.g., recruiting, handling grievances). However, with the exception of the six cases mentioned, the recruitment of staff was from inside the organization, emphasizing a knowledge of personnel administration rather than equal employment expertise. Finally, the lack of expertise on equal employment problems was most apparent in small companies with no affiliation with national minority group employment programs.

These observations on staff suggest an administrative question that was discussed in a number of the executive interviews: Should the company establish a separate administrative unit to handle equal employment policy and activities? One might argue that such a step would be a major administrative and resource commitment to the equalizing of opportunities. However, only two of the executive respondents favored such a step. It was clear that the other executives assumed that equalizing opportunities could best be accomplished in their companies by administering these practices within the framework of present employment structure, either adding new duties to current departmental functions or developing existing policies and practices. The arguments against a separate administrative structure were threefold. First, it would separate the responsibility of equalizing opportunities from individual units and assign it to a group outside of these units; it was felt that this might result in making the program remote to most units. Second, the creation of such a unit would be expensive in money, time and resources, and few of the respondents felt such a step could be justified by present company economics. Finally, most of the respondents felt that the practices of equal employment opportunity should be rooted in everyday, normal employment procedures with the eventual goal of treating Negro employment no differently from any other employment. Many of the current equal employment practices, particularly in recruitment, were regarded as temporary or transitional measures to the inclusion of Negroes in normal employment procedures. These respondents felt that a separate administrative unit might prolong the transitional period to normal employment procedures and continue needless separate treatment of Negro job applicants.

(3) The responsibility structure. There were some variations in the responsibility structure of equal employment activities. In twelve of the companies, the major responsibility for the program was directly under a vice-president in personnel or industrial

relations. In two other cases, responsibility was in the hands of a coordinate committee of executive officers who represented a major department of operations in the company. In the remaining cases, equal employment activities were under the direction of junior officers or administrative aides to senior officers. Several propositions about responsibility were suggested in our executive interviews:

(a) The individual charged with the responsibility for equal employment practices should report directly and frequently to the senior officer of the company. This was apparent in twelve companies. In two cases, the individuals responsible for equal employment practices reported directly to the board of directors at scheduled meetings. Apparently, such access to top officers gives these activities and the person who administers them a sense of importance and urgency in company priorities.

(b) Lines of responsibility should be developed directly between local plant personnel involved in equal employment policies and their corporate counterparts. This involves considerable difficulty in most companies because the local representative is part of another responsibility structure that might be violated by direct contact between corporate and local personnel. In the majority of companies in this study, the local personnel were responsible to local authorities for administering the program and had minimal contact with their corporate counterparts.

The responsibility structure for these activities in most of the companies followed traditional administrative practices of the company.

(4) The structure of the control or auditing system. It was clear that none of the companies had audited minority group employment practices or made inventories of Negro workers before the advent of outside intervention from state or federal agencies or voluntary membership in a national minority group employment program. In the defense-linked industries, the reporting form for federal agencies in contract compliance was the basic auditing tool, although in a few companies corporate headquarters required information beyond that required on the report (e.g., promotion rates for Negroes). There were variations among the companies in the use of the auditing form. One Midwest company requires local plant officials to use the form as discussion material for interdepartmental meetings on minority group employment. In another company, the material in the form is used to review plant progress at corporate meetings. The following observations about auditing should be noted:

(a) The extent to which use is made of auditing forms as the basis for correcting discriminatory practices in the local plant is a reflection of both the emphasis placed on auditing by corporate headquarters and who reviews the auditing forms. In the companies in which the audit was reviewed by the president or his immediate staff, a practice in six of the twenty companies, a considerable number of equal employment activities, particularly in recruitment, had been initiated.

(b) Considerably more progress in initiating equal employment activities is apparent in plants with highly formalized auditing systems than in plants where auditing is largely informal. In a large manufacturing plant in the Midwest, the plant supervisor requires a unit audit, department by department. He was thus able to plot progress in each unit of the company. He also feels that this system of auditing involves more personnel in the company diagnosis of employment practices.

(c) The frequency of audit is usually set by the requirements of the outside agency, although six of the companies had more frequent audits than were required. Apparently, the frequency of audits reflects certain company philosophies about control; in the companies with centralized control, auditing in all activities including equal employment was more frequent than in the companies with decentralized control. Thus, the administrative network of the company sets the limits within which auditing takes place.

(5) Evaluation effectiveness. It seems clear that there are both similarities and differences in evaluating the effectiveness of equal employment opportunity practices in the twenty companies in this study. First, corporate-based respondents were more inclined than local plant respondents to use multiple criteria to evaluate effectiveness (e.g., the number of Negro employees, the number of Negro applicants, the number of Negro promotions, extent of placement in previously all-white departments). In contrast, local plant personnel placed more emphasis on a single criterion--the size of the Negro work force in the plant. In both groups, number criteria loomed large.

It is also clear that different referents were used to characterize affirmative action in the twenty companies. This resulted largely from differences in employment structure. Thus, in one company, the Negro-to-white worker ratio was used as a guide to progress; in another, considerable emphasis was placed on the employment of a young Negro woman in a previously all-white secretarial office.

## Problems in the Administration of
## Equal Employment Opportunities

What are some of the administrative problems encountered in the application of equal employment policies and practices? There are four problem areas that deserve special attention:

corporate-local plant relations; the structure of the employment policy; relations with federal and state agencies; and union-management relations.

(1) <u>Corporate-local plant relations</u>. Several problems deriving from corporate-local plant relations were obvious in discussion with both corporate and local plant respondents. As a general rule, the corporate headquarters developed general policy and guidelines to be practiced at the local plant level. The extent to which practices were enacted was apparently a function of two factors: (a) the degree of centralized control over local options exercised by corporate headquarters and (b) the ordering of priorities at the local plant level. Companies differ in the degree of control over local operations and procedures. In some companies, the degree of control over local operations is extensive, with little flexibility left in the hands of the local plant personnel. An electric manufacturing company in the Midwest is typical of this mode of control. An extensive series of operating manuals has been developed to cover sixteen major activity areas in local plant operations (including equal employment practices). A comprehensive equal employment program is evident in this company, touching all of the activity area emphasized in this study. Executive rewards and promotions are based on the extent to which the "book has been followed."[2] At the other extreme is the company in which authority and decision-making has been completely decentralized to local personnel. A national chain of retail food stores follows this practice with all employment decisions at the local level. Few equal employment practices have been developed in the branch units of this company. There has been considerable resistance to corporate initiative in the program. Contrary to the centralized company discussed above, the communication patterns between corporate and local management on equal employment opportunities were quite poor, and in two local establishments where the store managers were acquainted with company policy on the program, they were not able to give any specifics of the programs, nor had any equalizing practices been initiated. In both of the cases discussed, traditions in administrative control patterns shaped the effectiveness of corporate efforts on the local level.

Several respondents from corporate headquarters reported that traditional practices of local autonomy in plant operations limited their efforts in developing equal employment activities.

---

[2]It is also evident in this company that this system of control extends from local headquarters to departmental units. Although the final approval for hiring an employee rests with the department head, the manual specifically guides his decisions, making nonrational rejection of a qualified candidate subject to executive scrutiny.

It seemed obvious that, when decision-making was highly decentralized, corporate staff personnel were mainly advisory in local equal employment activities. The company's major efforts were confined to "fighting local brushfires." For their part, local plant personnel in highly autonomous plants viewed the problem of equal employment with some detachment, labeling it "more of a corporate problem than one that affects this plant." The local autonomy of units made it difficult in many cases for corporate staff to transmit a sense of purpose and urgency on equal employment to local staff personnel and to elicit from them a positive response to this appeal.

It was also clear from the interviews with corporate and local plant personnel that priorities given to equal employment activities differed from corporate staff to local plant personnel. Corporate executives tended to give equal employment activities a priority not shared generally by local plant officials. On the local plant level, equal employment activities competed with a range of other activities, and, inevitably, matters of plant operation, sales and collective bargaining were given higher priority. Equal employment practices were regarded by many local personnel as a "crisis in priorities," demanding resources (time, talent and money) that had to be diverted from basic operations of the plant unit. With few exceptions, these local personnel did not regard equal employment activities as a basis on which unit performance would be evaluated by corporate headquarters. It was believed that traditional criteria (efficiency of operation, profits and growth) were still the yardsticks by which unit performance would be judged.[3] Equal employment activities were viewed by some as a diversion that could be afforded only in a period of profitable business operations.

(2) The structure of the employment policy. Another problem in the development of equal employment activities was imposed by the employment policies of some companies. A large retail chain store had the following provisions in its employment policy that made it difficult to initiate equal employment activities. All new full-time employees must have a high school education; employees are hired for career potential in the company (i.e., they must have the background and experience to go beyond entry jobs); all promotions into higher-level jobs must be from within the ranks of the company; store manager must have served an apprenticeship at a prescribed number of jobs in the company; the job applicant must be able to pass with a score of 70 or higher a standard arithmetic test; and the final decision to hire is a joint decision between

---

[3]It should be noted that where corporate headquarters had made an attempt to redefine criteria for performance by including equal employment activities, considerable effort in this area was generated by the local unit.

department head and store manager. Almost half of the company work force are half-time employees, but seniority does not accrue to half-time workers, nor is it any guarantee of promotion to full-time work status. These provisions have existed without change for a number of years and certainly make it difficult to develop equal employment practices.

Although all of the provisions of employment policies of the companies in this study were subject to change, there was some variation in how frequently they were reviewed and how many changes were made. Generally, companies that had a flexible policy in content and change provisions were more likely than other companies to initiate extensive equal employment practices.

(3) Relations with federal and state agencies. It was clear that one source of discontent among corporate and local-based personnel was the nature of company relations with federal and state agencies. The most frequent complaint made was the lack of coordination between state and federal agencies in dealing with the company. A large transportation concern was involved for three years in litigation on a single discrimination grievance. During this period, the company was involved at different times with the local city human relations agency, the state fair employment practices commission, the Civil Rights Commission and the federal compliance Air Force officer. The company complained on three counts. It was necessary to submit a completely new legal brief for each hearing, causing considerable expense in time, money and legal talent; there was little contact among the agencies; and the results of past hearings in which the company was successful seemed to matter little. These complaints were echoed by a majority of the executive respondents. A vice-president of an electronics company complained that multiple grievance procedures available to the complainant could involve the company in extensive litigation without just cause; an unscrupulous worker could threaten the company with these actions. All of the executive respondents were agreed that revisions in company-agency relationships were necessary.

(4) Union-management relations. In the companies with union contracts, corporate respondents reported that provisions of the contract were frequent barriers to the development of certain equal employment activities. The following points were noted:

(a) Moving Negroes into apprenticible trade jobs usually meant increasing the number of these jobs. Most contracts strictly define the radios of apprentices to journeymen, and any change would have to be negotiated through intensive collective bargaining.

(b) Moving Negroes into certain categories of jobs frequently required renegotiation of the lines of job progression and seniority provisions in the contract.

Therefore, some opportunities for equalizing employment depend to a large extent on the ability to renegotiate key contract clauses.

CHAPTER **5** INTERPERSONAL RELATIONS
AND THE APPLICATION OF
NONDISCRIMINATORY EMPLOY-
MENT PRACTICES

The application of a nondiscrimination policy in a company, or any organization, cannot be assessed without reference to the experiences and attitudes of the Negro and white workers involved. It is a sociological principle of long standing that directives, policy changes and new application procedures of management are mediated through a complex network of social relationships involving work and nonwork statuses, as well as supervisor-worker and co-worker experiences. There are three reasons why it is necessary to examine the experiences and attitudes of Negro and white workers in companies that initiate a nondiscrimination policy or a program of affirmative action in minority group employment. First, such policies and programs are designed to modify existing employment practices and the behavior and attitudes of the workers in the company. Some practices may be initiated to change the experiences of Negro workers (e.g., increase their mobility or training). Other practices may be designed to increase the Negro worker's confidence in bidding for promotions or training opportunities. Still other practices may be initiated to create a more positive image of Negro workers for the whites employed in the company. It is only by talking to the workers on different levels of employment that it becomes possible to assess the effects, if any, of these changes. The fact that the practices have been initiated may be of little significance if worker attitudes and behavior have not been modified.

A second reason to concern ourselves with workers is the fact that workers themselves may influence or modify the intent of a given management directive. The company may be genuinely interested in developing more promotions and training opportunities for Negroes, but the work environment--the constellation of attitudes, behaviors and traditions that characterizes all work situations--may facilitate or hinder these goals depending on the friendliness or hostility of Negro-white relationships. In some cases, white workers can influence the extent of informal training of Negroes by varying degrees of cooperation or antagonism. At times, Negro workers may find themselves victimized by the tight, in-group organization of white workers, cliques and informal friendships that influence promotions, training and the recruitment of new workers. The need to observe workers as active modifiers of policy makes a consideration of worker attitudes and experiences a necessary part of an assessment of equal employment opportunity practice.

Finally, much of the resistance to change in minority group employment practices is predicated or rationalized on managerial beliefs that white workers would resist such changes. It is necessary to assess the validity of this argument as well as to map the patterns of white worker reactions and resistance to changes in minority group employment practices.

Some students of minority group employment feel that such an emphasis on worker reactions is unnecessary. They subscribe to the "bid and forbid" theory of management which says, in effect, that decisions and policies implemented by the managerial elite of a company are translated into complementary practices at the operational level. In this context, it becomes necessary only to ascertain the thinking and future planning of the top company executives to make some predictions about the future directions of minority group employment. The workers thus become passive actors in the administration of policy.

Furthermore, in detailing the lessons to be learned from management experiences, these observers find it necessary only to describe the decision-making process of the management elite, the alternatives considered in policy formulation and the pattern of administration relationships that support the policy. The reactions of the workers and their view of the policy is considered of little importance; and yet one could argue that these are important dimensions of the information process of organizations that undertake new practices in minority group employment. One cannot deny the importance of corporate and local plant decision-making to an understanding of minority group employment practices, but such data must be seen as the opening chapters of a book of events in which the behavior and attitudes of the workers form an important concluding chapter. An administrative review of company practices is an incomplete statement of information and is certainly no substitute for an analysis of the network of behavior and attitudes that constitute worker reactions to nondiscrimination policy.

## THE LIMITATIONS OF THE SAMPLE

We have already noted in Chapter 1 that an analysis of white and Negro worker groups in this study precluded any statistically rigorous comparisons. Although both groups were characterized by a high nonresponse rate, the factors making for nonresponse among Negroes were apparently different than among whites. Second, in order to increase the size of the Negro response group, eighteen months or more of service was used as a criterion for the inclusion of a Negro worker in the sample group, whereas, among white workers, thirty-six months or more of service was used as the inclusion mark. Finally, in some of the more specialized job categories--professional, technical and administrative--there were few Negroes, making a comparison between whites and Negroes in these categories statistically impossible.

These shortcomings of the response groups suggest caution in reporting and interpretation of the observations. We concluded that, although direct statistical comparisons were of little value, the two sets of separate observations--one on the Negro group and the other on the white group--yielded a number of insights and hypotheses about the impact of company equal employment practices on the workers involved. In turn, these insights and hypotheses would become the basis of more research, which would utilize rigorous statistical controls.

## THE WHITE WORKER AND EQUAL EMPLOYMENT OPPORTUNITIES

The occupational specialties of the white workers in the sample were divided into four broad occupational categories: the white-collar specialized, including professionals, technicians and managers; the white-collar routine, including secretaries, business machine operators, switchboard operators, sales and low-skilled clerical; the blue-collar skilled, including apprenticeable trades only--electricians, machinists; and the blue-collar, low-skilled, including semiskilled, unskilled and service workers. The white response sample as a group were weighted toward skilled and white-collar work; 72 per cent of the white workers were employed in jobs other than "blue-collar low-skilled," with roughly one half of the group in white-collar routine jobs[1]  (see Table 3).

### The White Worker Views Negro Job Opportunities

Several themes seem apparent from the response patterns of white workers in this study:

(1) Few whites feel that the Negro has job problems because of skin color.

---

[1]Although the comparison may have little meaning, the Negro group was predominantly "blue-collar low-skilled" (79 per cent).

TABLE 3

OCCUPATIONAL DISTRIBUTION OF
WHITE RESPONDENTS IN STUDY

|  | Number | Percentage |
|---|---|---|
| White-collar specialized[a] | 33 | 16 |
| White-collar routine[b] | 94 | 46 |
| Blue-collar skilled[c] | 21 | 10 |
| Blue-collar low-skilled[d] | 57 | 28 |
| Total | 205 | 100% |

[a] Professionals, technicians and managers.

[b] Secretaries, business machine operators, switchboard operators, salespeople, low-skilled clerical.

[c] Apprenticeable trades.

[d] Semiskilled, unskilled and service jobs.

(2) Most whites feel that Negroes have the same job opportunities as anyone else and deny that prejudice or discrimination operate in the case of Negroes.

(3) Most whites seem puzzled by apparent Negro militancy in pressuring for jobs through civil rights activity.

(4) Most whites appear to share a basic acceptance of Negro employment both in northern and southern locations but feel that Negroes are getting or will get special treatment, favors or preference on jobs, resulting in increasing disadvantage for whites.

(5) Few of the whites feel that the Negro should be denied the right to a job if he has the ability, but there is widespread agreement that only an occasional Negro has the ability.

(6) There is a widespread feeling among whites that the Negro is less prepared for work and promotions than whites; this lack of preparation is blamed on the Negro himself and his family or associations, rather than on the community or society as a whole.

(7) Most whites see the solution to the problem of equalizing opportunities in having the Negro "help himself" (more education, more training, developing better motivation).

A common summary of feelings and attitudes was found in the comments of a 41-year old machinist helper who said:

> The Negro has a right to a good job because he has a family to support like white men.   Live and let live is what I say. Even if we don't like them (Negroes), we can work with them. I won't drink beer with one or have him to my house, but if he can do the job, ...that's all that counts.

> I know a lot of older Negroes, and they don't cause trouble. It is the young ones that are in the riots that worry me. They want everything too fast, and they don't care who gets hurt. Some of them are Commies.

A semiskilled steel worker in his thirties expressed similar sentiments, but added:

> Everything you read now says the Negro is treated unfairly in jobs and in housing. I don't think it's that bad. If they were kept down, it was their own fault. You can only get ahead by hard work, and if the Negro works hard, he'll do all right like everyone else.

## Separate Lines of Progression

In order to ascertain whether Negroes performed the same job activities as whites in similar job classifications, the following question was asked:  "Consider your present job for the moment. Do you feel that your activities in the job are the same as those of a Negro worker in the same job in the company?" Slightly more than half of the white workers reported knowledge of a Negro in the same job classification as their own, and, in this group, nine out of every ten workers reported that Negroes performed the same activities as white workers in similar jobs. In their view, there was nothing to indicate differential assignment of activities that would make the content of the same job different for Negroes.[2]

---

[2]This does not mean that such differences did not exist, but rather that few white workers perceived them to exist. This subtle difference between fact and perceived fact as reported by white respondents is important.

Training

     Only 45 of the 205 white worker respondents reported that there were any special training programs sponsored by their companies at the present time (tuition-sponsored or institutional instruction). Another 60 per cent of the sample reported that there were informal, on-the-job training programs in their companies; the job-holder gained new skills through natural skill accretion rather than planned instruction. Regardless of the type of training involved, only 12 of the 168 respondents who reported training programs felt that there was any difficulty for Negroes to gain admission into training if they were qualified. Of the 12 dissenters, 8 felt that Negroes would not be admitted to sales training or supervisory training, whereas the other 4 doubted that Negroes could be admitted to apprenticeable trade programs. The large majority of the whites felt that race was not a factor in admission to training and that seniority, merit and "luck" were the primary considerations. Eight of the whites reported incidents in which they felt race had been a positive influence in admitting a Negro to training; the company had "gone out of its way to get colored people into those jobs."

     These observations about white perspectives on race and training may be examined in another way. We asked the white respondents, "Suppose that a young Negro asked your advice about going to work for this company. He was interested in opportunities for training and promotion. What would you tell him?' Three-quarters of the white respondents reported that they would advise a Negro to take a job with their company. Among the 52 dissenters, there seemed to be common belief that training and promotions in their company were hard to come by for whites or Negroes and that the job situations in these areas offered few possibilities. It should be noted, however, that almost 80 per cent of the white workers disclaimed any knowledge of "differences" in opportunity in their companies for whites or Negroes, and the remaining 20 per cent of the group reported that it would be hard to advise a Negro applicant because they were not acquainted with any Negroes.

     The picture that emerges from these response patterns is one that details few problems for Negroes on the job. Although some respondents reported personal dislike of Negroes, few of them seemed inclined to deny Negroes jobs in their company or to quit the company in protest over the hiring of Negroes throughout the company or in their departments. What do these response patterns mean? Is there truly an acceptance of the Negro in the work place and equality of opportunity, or did white respondents assume a posture in these interviews that was contrary to the real situation? Although the data in this study cannot conclusively answer these questions, the following possibilities are suggested. It may well be that the normative is to accept Negro employment as a fact of life, regardless of personal feelings. There was repeated evidence in our interviews that white workers felt they did not have it within their power to reverse Negro employment trends and, thus, were willing to accept the situation. There was also some evidence that many whites did not regard Negroes as a personal or economic threat. Among younger workers, there was a general acceptance of Negroes in the job, to some extent a possible reflection of favorable, or at least neutral, past associations with Negroes in the Armed Services or in school. These observations suggest that there may have been a change in the climate of acceptance of Negroes in the work situation. This optimism must be tempered, however. It is likely that it has become normative to deny that employment inequality exists and, particularly in a period of national civil rights protest, to refrain from voicing one's true feelings on Negro employment. The high nonresponse rate among white workers may also indicate that the white worker group is biased toward the worker who is less likely to deny equality to Negro workers. Although these are all interesting possibilities, our data cannot be conclusive in suggesting definitive answers.

## The White Worker and Knowledge of Equal Employment Policies and Practices

For equal employment policies and practices to be effective, Negro and white workers must have knowledge of them and accept them. Undoubtedly, the public stance of the company on equal employment is an important consideration in equalizing opportunities, but also important is whether the worker recognizes this stance and accepts it as an ideal and guideline for behavior at work. To what extent were equal employment policies and practices known to white workers in the twenty companies studied?

The white workers in this study were asked, "Does this company have an equal employment policy for Negroes?" If the respondent answered affirmatively, he was asked, "Can you tell me something about this policy?" The answers to this question are tabulated in Table 4.

There are a number of striking observations about the data in Table 4. Knowledge about equal employment policies and practices was highest in the white-collar specialized group and lowest in the blue-collar unskilled group. Of the 205 white respondents in the study, 121 of them were aware that the company had an equal employment policy. This means that 41 per cent of the white respondents were unaware that their company had such a policy. Even among those who knew that the company had an equal employment policy, 57 respondents, 47 per cent, were unable to give a single detail of the policy or specific practices. The group least informed were in the lowest ranks of the company, and only 3 out of 57 respondents in this group were aware of a company equal employment policy.

## TABLE 4

### RELATIONSHIP BETWEEN OCCUPATIONAL CATEGORIES OF WHITE RESPONDENTS AND KNOWLEDGE OF EQUAL EMPLOYMENT POLICIES

| "Does this company have an equal employment policy for Negroes?" | Occupational Grouping[a] | | | |
|---|---|---|---|---|
| | White-collar specialized | White-collar routine | Blue-collar skilled | Blue-collar low-skilled |
| Yes | 97% | 80% | 50% | 6% |
| No | 3 | 20 | 50 | 56 |
| Don't know | -- | -- | -- | 38 |
| Total | 100% | 100% | 100% | 100% |
| Total number of respondents | 33 | 94 | 21 | 57 |

102

|  | Occupational Grouping[a] | | | |
| Number of details specified by respondents who reported that company had policy | White-collar specialized | White-collar routine | Blue-collar skilled | Blue-collar low-skilled |
| --- | --- | --- | --- | --- |
| 0 | 25% | 52% | 75% | b |
| 1 | 10 | 30 | 10 | |
| 2 | 15 | 16 | 15 | |
| 3 or more | 50 | 2 | -- | |
| | — | — | — | |
| Total | 100% | 100% | 100% | |
| Total number of respondents | 32 | 75 | 11 | 3 |

[a]See Table 3 for occupational definitions.

[b]Insufficient number of cases for percentages.

These findings suggest the following. First, personnel in these companies as a group were only moderately informed about company policy and practice. This low level of information may mean that company mechanisms for communicating policy are ineffective for a large proportion of workers, especially in the lower occupational groupings or that workers place a relatively low priority on obtaining information on equal employment policies and practices. Second, a large number of workers are neither inhibitors, facilitators or participants in policy and practices since they are apparently unaware of them.[3]   It is apparent that, in some cases, worker knowledge of policy and practice may make application difficult, whereas, in other cases, worker cooperation is predicated on some knowledge of policy. Although our observations strongly suggest that, in a large number of cases, white workers are passive agents in the administration of equal employment practices, this does not necessarily mean that equal employment practices are not being actively applied. The administration of equal employment practices in a community is not predicated on the knowledge and participation of white workers as may be the case in other policy applications (e.g., shared incentive plans). Managers retain the right to manage and develop practices and policies without the consent or participation of their workers. Management organization is essentially an authority organization, and worker compliance to policy is required by conditions of work rather than being sought through democratic appeals for compliance.

## Attitudes Toward Company Policy

While we have indicated that a large number of workers had no knowledge of equal employment policies or practices, it is nevertheless true that over one half of the workers did know that a policy existed. How did these workers feel about the policy? The white respondents who reported knowledge of a policy were asked the following two questions:   "How do you feel about the company's nondiscrimination policy?" and   "Do you think it was

---

[3]The extent to which white workers should be informed of company policies and practices was considered open to question by a number of executive respondents.   A local plant executive from a large manufacturing firm reported that workers in his company were informed selectively about equal employment policies and practices.   Informational emphasis was placed on the general posture of his company rather than on detailing on specific practices such as selection, recruitment and training.   This same respondent felt that "you only stir up trouble when you give this problem too much exposure to workers, and in some cases a little ignorance on the part of the workers actually helps to facilitate the application of the policies."

a mistake for the company to adopt a nondiscrimination policy?" These data are summarized in Table 5.

The data in this table indicate the following. About two respondents out of every three voiced approval of the policy, but the highest measure of approval was among respondents in the white-collar specialized group. Among workers in white-collar routine jobs, about one half approved of the policy. None of the blue-collar skilled workers favored it. This same pattern is apparent when we asked whether it was a mistake for the company to adopt the policy.

The response patterns in the white-collar routine group deserves special comment. This is a category composed of diverse occupational types; if the size of the group was larger, we might find that the differences within this category were greater than between the category and the other groupings. Nevertheless, two distinct types of employees are recognizable in this category: workers who were bureaucratically oriented in their jobs (i.e., well-defined duties, close supervision and subject to extensive paper control) and workers who were entrepreneurally oriented (i.e., variable duties, little supervision and little, usually remote, paper control). The first group of workers usually shares a precise division of labor within some large organization--for example, the clerical staff in a large office. The second group of workers are in jobs where emphasis is on personal initiative and freedom from a precise division of labor (e.g., field salesworkers, service representatives). Given these two types of workers, what differences, if any, were apparent in attitudes toward company equal employment policy?

This question cannot be answered by our data, but the results of a university-sponsored survey in one of the large companies in our sample yielded the following information. Using a sample of 646 workers, the study indicated that acceptance of a nondiscrimination policy is higher among the bureaucratically oriented than among the entrepreneurally oriented workers. The first group was also less likely to feel that the adoption of the policy was a mistake. This suggests that workers in jobs which allow freedom of choice to exercise alternate options and in which self-initiative and competition is high will be less accepting of equal employment policies than other workers. Why might this be so? Again in the absence of specific data, we must speculate. First, workers in entrepreneurial roles retain considerable autonomy and initiative in structuring social relationships in work. The salesman on the road or the house-to-house service worker is not bound by the social and work relationships imposed by a fixed, closed work environment; nor is he subject to close supervision in the work situation. Second, he is likely to pride himself on being free of company "red tape" or controls that govern more bureaucratic jobs. Third, the nature of entrepreneurial work makes it less

## TABLE 5

### WHITE ATTITUDES TOWARD COMPANY NONDISCRIMINATION POLICY BY MAJOR OCCUPATIONAL CATEGORIES[a]

| 'How do you feel about company policy?' | White-collar specialized | White-collar routine | Blue-collar skilled | Blue-collar unskilled |
|---|---|---|---|---|
| Approve | 94% | 57% | -- | b |
| Disapprove | -- | 22 | 90% | |
| Undecided or don't know | 6 | 21 | 10 | |
| Total | 100% | 100% | 100% | 100% |
| Total number of respondents | 32 | 75 | 11 | 3 |

106

| "Was it a mistake for the company to adopt policy?" | White-collar specialized | White-collar routine | Blue-collar skilled | Blue-collar unskilled |
|---|---|---|---|---|
| Yes | -- | 66% | 100% | |
| No | 94% | 20 | -- | b |
| Undecided or don't know | 6 | 14 | -- | |
| Total | 100% | 100% | 100% | 100% |
| Total number of respondents | 32 | 75 | 11 | 3 |

aSee Table 3 for definitions of occupational categories.

bInsufficient cases for percentage distribution.

likely that the job-holder will accept imposed patterns of relationships, and his lack of acceptance is not subject to the same intense,
immediate reprimand as in the case of the bureaucratic job-holder.
Finally, workers in bureaucratically oriented jobs accept rules and
rule changes as part of the job, while the entrepreneurial worker
perceives rules and rule changes as attempts to restrict his individual
initiative or limit his autonomy. These remarks are speculative
and suggestive rather than explanatory. Hopefully, future research
will focus more attention on these two types of workers and how
their attitudes and behavior may influence equal employment policy
and practices.

### The White Worker and Interpersonal Relations at Work

Several themes concerning white-Negro worker interpersonal
work relations are apparent in the white worker interviews:

(1) Although Negroes and whites may interact on the job as
work associates, intimate forms of social contact (e.g., recreation,
extended conversation, seeking advice) are not very frequent. Only
six of the white workers reported knowing a Negro worker well
enough to regard him as "a close friend that you can talk over
confidential matters with" or "a good friend to whom you can say
what you really think." Five of these respondents were in the white-
collar specialized group of respondents.

(2) Very little social contact between Negroes and whites
occurs outside of work, the only exceptions being among professional
and technical workers.

(3) There are apparently networks of cliques among both whites
and Negroes, but mixed cliques were in evidence only in a few
cases. For the most part, Negro workers seek work associates
among other Negro workers, and whites select from within the
circle of white workers.

(4) One fifth of the white workers reported experience at work
that made them more favorable toward Negro workers. On the other
hand, only four white workers reported experiences that made them
feel less favorable toward Negroes.

(5) Company-sponsored social activities for workers are
usually mixed affairs. Only in one southern location did Negroes
organize their own social activities outside of company-wide
programs. But even in mixed events, relatively little contact
occurs between Negroes and whites.

(6) Only in two reported instances in different companies were
company-sponsored social activities canceled to avoid mixed events.

In one case, a bowling establishment objected to mixed bowling teams in the company league; the bowling nights were suspended for two weeks, continuing at another bowling establishment. In the second case, a company picnic was canceled because some of the white workers expressed resentment at the inclusion of Negroes.

How do patterns of interpersonal relations relate to equal opportunity practices? About half of the white respondents felt that chances for promotion were helped by being in the "right group," although there was general agreement that merit, hard work and seniority were more important considerations. There was less agreement that being in the right group influenced training opportunities or supervisor-worker relations; only one respondent out of every ten felt that this was the case. To a large extent, white workers downgraded the influence of group membership as an influence on opportunities in the companies. Greater reliance was placed on ability to do the job, personality, experience or luck The qualities considered crucial for white worker success were also reported by three quarters of the white respondents as crucial factors in Negro worker success. Whether these responses reflect an ideal or a reality was not clear from the data in this study.

### The White Worker Views the Negro Worker

An attempt was made in this study to assess the image of the Negro worker as seen through the eyes of white respondents. These images varied with the occupational status of the white respondent, but the data suggest a number of propositions regarding Negro-white relations in the work situation:

(1) The Negro is viewed as a cause of his misfortune rather than as a product of it. When asked the question, "There seem to be a lot of Negroes in unskilled jobs--why have these Negroes not been able to get better jobs?", three quarters of the white workers responded by blaming personal qualities of the Negro workers (e.g., low motivation, lack of intelligence, satisfaction with unskilled work, fear of responsible work). The Negro was viewed not as a victim of a network of institutional practices but rather as being personally responsible for his circumstances.

(2) Again, when asked, "What are some of the things that cause problems for Negro workers?", one half of the white respondents answered the question in terms of undesirable personal qualities of the Negro (e.g., bad social manners, lack of self-control, "a chip on the shoulder"). Few respondents viewed the cause of these problems as external to the Negro.

(3) Evaluations of Negro job performance varied. The performance of Negro professionals, administrators and technicians

was regarded highly by white co-workers. The work of Negro office workers was regarded as average, and a common point of criticism was failure to take responsibility or act decisively in minor matters. Among the white respondents, there was a tendency to view the Negro blue-collar worker as less capable than his white counterpart; two thirds of the white respondents held this view. Among white respondents in white-collar work, there was a tendency to reject categorizing a group of Negroes as "good or bad workers" and emphasize assessment of individual Negroes. By contrast, blue-collar workers were more willing to label groups of Negro workers as "good or bad workers." Seven out of every ten blue-collar respondents regarded the Negro's work potential as less than that of whites in comparable jobs. There was one area of broad agreement among all white workers--the belief that Negroes in unskilled or service work were less reliable than whites in these jobs.

Few of the white respondents admitted openly that Negroes have a special problem in employment. It was felt that Negroes with the right personal qualities can progress and that these qualities are essentially the same as those that move white workers ahead. At the same time, there was widespread admission that many Negroes do not have the qualities to get ahead and that this acts to limit their opportunities. The solution to this dilemma was not seen in company remedial programs or preferential treatment. Time and again, the unsolicited comment was, "If he is to be helped, the Negro must help himself." Although this solution was frequently given by white respondents, they verbalized few specific ways the Negro could achieve this self-help goal.

## THE NEGRO WORKER AND
## EQUAL EMPLOYMENT OPPORTUNITIES

The occupational specialties of the Negro workers in the sample were divided into four broad categories as in the case of the white workers: the white-collar specialized (professionals, technicians and managers); the white-collar routine (secretaries, business machine operators, salesworkers and low-skilled clerical); the blue-collar skilled (apprenticeable trades only--electricians, machinists); and the blue-collar low-skilled (semiskilled, unskilled and service workers). As a group, the Negro response sample was weighted toward the blue-collar unskilled; 79 per cent of the Negro respondents were in this group, whereas only 14 per cent were in white-collar jobs (see Table 6). While there is a marked difference in occupational distribution between the Negro and white workers (see Table 3), caution must be used in assessing the significance of this fact; there was a high nonresponse rate in both groups. The observations to be made, as in the case of the white workers, should be regarded as suggestive rather than definitive reference points for research among white and Negro workers.

## TABLE 6

### OCCUPATIONAL DISTRIBUTION OF
### NEGRO RESPONDENTS IN STUDY

|  | Number | Percentage |
|---|---|---|
| White-collar specialized | 10 | 4 |
| White-collar routine | 20 | 10 |
| Blue-collar skilled | 15 | 7 |
| Blue-collar low-skilled | 170 | 79 |
| Total | 215 | 100% |

The Negro Worker Views Negro Job Opportunities

Several themes seem apparent from the response patterns of Negro workers in this study.

There was considerable variation in the perception of opportunities among Negro respondents. As a group, the ten Negroes in professional, technical and administrative jobs regarded their opportunities within the companies as good, and two of them felt that high executive positions within the company were possible. None of these ten respondents felt that their jobs were token; they regarded their work as a real contribution to the company. Only two of these ten felt that race had been a factor in their employment with the company, and these two respondents were in the personnel department with job duties largely confined to minority group employment problems. All ten of these respondents reported high satisfaction with their jobs and indicated that they planned to continue in such employment.

Negro respondents in office and sales work were less enthused about future job prospects but felt that these jobs were considerably better than most jobs in which their friends and relatives worked. Seven of the twenty respondents in this group felt that race had been an important factor in initial employment and that they had received aid in obtaining these jobs from Negro social agencies or Negro professionals. Little thought had been given in this group to job advancement; considerably more emphasis was placed on job security. Opinions varied in this group as to whether their jobs were token, but only two respondents reported that they perceived their jobs as showpieces.

Among the fifteen blue-collar skilled workers, there was general satisfaction with the job. Seven of the respondents who were journeymen felt that they had worked harder than whites to attain this status. The eight apprentices felt that they would become journeymen in normal progression through the craft, although one of the apprentices reported that he would attend a technical school for more specialized training to obtain employment outside of the craft. All but two of the respondents in the group felt that race was a factor in opportunities and that work assignments in less desirable jobs had been given to them in the past. However, there was no inclination to downgrade the special attractions of craft jobs (wages, work conditions), and twelve of the respondents reported that craft employment offered better opportunity to get ahead than most jobs for Negro workers.

The least satisfaction with jobs was found in the blue-collar unskilled group. Of the 170 workers in this group, 89 of them expressed dissatisfaction with their present jobs, and 115 of them saw no real chance for advancement. Only 8 workers in this group felt that they might have supervisory jobs some day. The most important barriers to job mobility reported by these respondents were their race and their lack of access to training and background preparation. Only 26 of these respondents felt, however, that race was the most significant barrier to job mobility. It was felt by 152 respondents in this group that with training they could progress in their work; only 3 of these felt optimistic that new training opportunities would develop for them. A chronic complaint in this group was that companies recruited outside for new Negro employees to staff the more skilled jobs, thus bypassing long-service Negro employees who could do the work if given a chance.[4]

---

[4]In a number of interviews with local plant executives in these companies, this point was discussed. These executives felt that "retreading" long-service employees for skilled jobs was expensive in terms of company resources (time, money, talent). Furthermore, pressures from compliance officers and civil rights action groups required immediate staffing of Negroes in skilled jobs, making it impossible to engage in lengthy retraining efforts for long-service employees and necessary to recruit Negroes from the outside to fill these jobs.

## THE NEGRO WORKER AND INFORMATION
## OF EQUAL EMPLOYMENT POLICY

It has already been indicated in an earlier section of this chapter that a sizable proportion of white respondents in this study had little or no information about the existence of an equal employment policy and procedures. To what extent were Negroes knowledgeable in these areas? It might be assumed that Negroes would have a greater vested interest in the possession of such knowledge. As in the case of whites, we asked the Negroes, ''Does this company have an equal employment opportunity policy for Negroes?'' If the response was affirmative, we asked, ''Can you give me some of the details of this policy?'' The responses to these questions are tabulated in Table 7.

The data in this table show that approximately one Negro worker in four had knowledge of the company problem in equal employment opportunities. The blue-collar unskilled group was the least informed. Only 20 per cent of the 170 workers in this group knew about the existence of the policy, whereas 51 per cent of the 45 higher-skilled Negroes were knowledgeable. When asked about specific practices, 29 of the 61 Negroes who had knowledge of the program (47 per cent), could not identify a single practice. These observations indicate that the level of information in equal employment policy and practices was extremely low among our Negro respondents.

When asked for information on specific recruiting, training and promotion practices aimed at reducing Negro disadvantagement, our Negro respondents again evidenced a low level of information:

(1) The Negro respondents were asked, ''Has the company done anything special about trying to hire more Negro workers?'' Of the 215 Negro respondents, 87 per cent answered ''don't know'' to this question; 10 per cent who answered the question affirmatively could give no details about company recruitment of Negroes.

(2) The Negro respondents were asked, ''Has the company done anything special to improve opportunities for Negro workers?'' Three quarters of the Negro respondents answered this question with a negative or ''don't know''; 8 per cent who answered this question affirmatively could give no details about special measures to improve conditions.

(3) The Negro respondents were asked, ''Has the company done anything out of the ordinary to bring job openings to the attention of Negroes?'' Two thirds of the 215 Negro respondents reported a lack of awareness of any such special attempts.

## TABLE 7

## RELATIONSHIP BETWEEN OCCUPATIONAL CATEGORIES OF NEGRO RESPONDENTS AND KNOWLEDGE OF EQUAL EMPLOYMENT POLICIES

| "Does this company have an equal employment policy for Negroes?" | Occupational Grouping[a] | | | |
| --- | --- | --- | --- | --- |
| | White-collar specialized | White-collar routine | Blue-collar skilled | Blue-collar low-skilled |
| Yes | 90% | 40% | 66% | 20% |
| No | -- | 10 | -- | 10 |
| Don't know | 10 | 50 | 33 | 70 |
| Total | 100% | 100% | 100% | 100% |
| Total number of respondents | 10 | 20 | 15 | 170 |

114

Occupational Grouping [a]

| Number of details specified by respondents who reported that the company had policy | White-collar specialized | White-collar routine | Blue-collar skilled | Blue-collar low-skilled |
|---|---|---|---|---|
| 0 | -- | 50% | 50% | 60% |
| 1 | -- | 25 | 50 | 30 |
| 2 | 100% | -- | -- | 10 |
| 3 or more | -- | 25 | -- | -- |
| Total | 100% | 100% | 100% | 100% |
| Total number of respondents | 9 | 8 | 10 | 34 |

[a] See Table 3 for occupational definitions.

It seems clear from these observations that equal employment policy and practices are not widely known among Negro respondents and tend to be remote from their job experiences. We cannot conclude from these observations, however, that the companies did either little or a great deal in equal employment problems. Our interviews with executive respondents indicate that various equal employment activities and practices were operative. Apparently, few Negroes were aware of them or know of them in any detail, a significant barrier to the development of a climate of equal opportunity within the company.

## THE NEGRO WORKER VIEWS
## EQUAL EMPLOYMENT OPPORTUNITY

How did the Negro view equal employment opportunities in the company setting? Did he feel that the company was making a major effort? Did he feel that the position of Negroes in the work situation had improved? The response patterns of Negro workers give some clue to the answers to these questions:

(1) The Negro respondents were asked, ''How much effort do you think the top management of this company is making to improve opportunities for Negro workers?'' Of 45 Negro respondents in jobs other than blue-collar unskilled, 42 reported that the company was making an effort to improve opportunities; only 30 of the 170 blue-collar unskilled workers felt this way. The evidence given for this view varied, as demonstrated in Table 8. Apparently, among all workers who shared this view, the principal evidence was increased employment of Negroes. Among blue-collar skilled and white-collar workers, the other important sources of evidence were job improvement for the Negroes, personal experience of self or friends or company advertising. These indicators ranked close to each other, while among the blue-collar unskilled, evidence based on company advertising was the only other important source of evidence.

(2) We also asked the Negro respondents, ''How about your immediate supervisor? How interested do you think he is in improving opportunities for Negro workers in this company?'' Of the 215 respondents, 189 confessed ignorance of their supervisor's attitude on the subject; 9 respondents felt that their supervisor was not interested or was hostile to equalizing opportunities; and 17 respondents reported that their supervisor was interested in equalizing opportunities.

(3) The Negro respondents were asked, ''When you first came here, did you feel that the company was making an effort to improve opportunities for Negro workers in this company?'' and ''Do you still

feel that way now?'' About one third of the Negro workers felt that the company was trying to improve opportunities for Negroes when they first came to work, and 55 per cent of the group felt that the company was doing so at the present time. Among those who saw an increase in company effort to improve opportunities, increased employment of Negroes, elimination of segregated facilities and company advertising on job equality were cited as the main indicators of change.

(4) Among Negro respondents who felt that the company was making a major effort to improve opportunities and who saw increasing efforts along these lines, the motives of management are suspect. Asked, ''Why are they doing this?,'' the seventy Negro respondents who saw evidence of company efforts answered:

(a) Pressure from an outside agency, group or person--government or civil rights group (90 per cent of the group reported this as a motive).

TABLE 8

NEGRO EVALUATION OF COMPANY
NONDISCRIMINATION EFFORTS

| Evidence for Improvement | White-Collar and Blue-Collar Skilled Number of respondents    42 | Blue-Collar Unskilled Number of respondents    30 |
|---|---|---|
| More Negroes employed now than before | 40 | 30 |
| More Negroes in better jobs than before | 42 | 11 |
| Equal employment poster or ad | 38 | 28 |
| Newspaper picture or story on company progress | 12 | 8 |
| Personal experience or experience of a friend | 39 | 12 |

(b) "Somebody made them do it" (39 per cent).

(c) Need for new manpower (38 per cent).

(d) The company is interested in Negro problems and wants to help solve them (4 per cent).

These are discrete observations, but they seem to imply the following. Most Negroes in this study did not perceive a work environment where major efforts were being made by company or supervisors to equalize opportunities.[5]   Even among those who perceived such efforts, the company motives were viewed as the product of coercive forces from outside the company rather than as voluntary. This suggests that company attempts to strengthen Negro worker morale through equalizing opportunities may frequently fail, not through a lack of effort on the company's part, but rather because this effort is viewed with suspicion by the workers.

### The Negro Worker and Exposure to Informal Work Experience

We have already noted that most of the companies in this study do not have formal training programs but utilize on-the-job work experiences to prepare their workers for more responsible jobs. It seems clear that informal work experiences are an important mechanism for enlarging the skills of the worker and making him more promotable. In many companies, informal work experiences may be the product of chance. For example, a worker may be absent from work for a few days, and another, less skilled worker may be asked to take his place. For the second man, such work assignments may be an opportunity to learn new skills that may become the basis of later promotion. Or a worker may be asked to help a more skilled worker on a job, thus permitting exposure to new skills that make the worker more valuable. In some cases, such exposure to informal job training may follow seniority lines or be rigorously defined by union contract. It seems clear, however, that, in most cases, supervisors or co-workers have great flexibility in choosing personnel to fill such assignments, and there is little doubt that these assignments are important considerations in increasing the promotability of the worker.

The question is posed:  Are Negroes bypassed in such opportunities for exposure to informal learning? In order to ascertain the answer to this question, we asked our white and Negro respondents the following three questions:

---

[5]This does not mean that such efforts were not under way, but rather that most Negroes were not aware of them.

(1) "On your present job, are you restricted to one kind of work, or do you have opportunities to learn other skills?"

(2) "Do you often get a chance to work at a job that involves more responsibility than your own?"

(3) "Do you often get a chance to trade jobs or fill in on jobs that give you an opportunity to become familiar with work that is different from your own?"

The answers to these questions are tabulated in Table 9.

These data indicate that such informal learning was the exception rather than the rule both among white and Negro respondents, but relatively more whites reported such experiences than Negroes. The existence of such discrepancies in informal learning opportunities was further substantiated by spontaneous comments from several Negro respondents:

> I have worked here five years as a sweeper and wanted to get on the bench (apprenticeable work). There must be fifteen new workers there, and all of them started where I am. They are white, and the older workers used them for help on the machines when there was a rush job. I couldn't move over there because I never got a chance to help out and get some experience.

> Some of the people here get used to relieve workers who are sick or absent. That gives them experience. It all comes down to whether they like you . . . White people get those breaks. I was used only once.

> When they are busy on a job, they need help. The white guy on the machine will use a white man every time.

> My supervisor told me to learn all I could by watching the other girls on the business machines. They help each other, but I think they'd get mad if I asked them anything.

> This was a white man's factory, and maybe I'm lucky to be in here. The way to get ahead is to have an old timer show you the machines. They won't do it for Negroes.

> I asked about working after hours on my time to learn some of the other jobs and machines, but the boss told me that I could only work with an experienced worker, and nobody wanted to stay.

These quotes, which give poignant testimony to a subtle form of discrimination in work, could be multiplied. More than any other feature of the work situation, this lack of exposure to informal job learning was described with bitterness and frustration by our unskilled Negro respondents. There was a tendency to view this exclusion as a reflection of interpersonal relations at work. Thus, two thirds of the 170 unskilled Negroes felt that promotion and training prospects were better if you were in the "right group," which was usually all white. We asked the unskilled Negroes, "In getting ahead in the job, what counts more for the Negro--hard work or being in with the right group?" "Hard work" was mentioned by 120 of the workers, but under closer probing, even these workers added that "the right group does not do any harm."

TABLE 9

OPPORTUNITIES FOR INFORMAL JOB EXPERIENCE
BY RACE (BLUE-COLLAR UNSKILLED WORKERS)

"On your present job, are you restricted to one kind of work, or do you have opportunities to learn other skills?"

|  | Restricted to One Job | Opportunities to Learn Other Skills | Total Number of Respondents |
|---|---|---|---|
| Whites | 63% | 37% | 57 |
| Negroes | 94 | 6 | 170 |

"Do you often get a chance to work at a job that involves more responsibility than your own?"

|  | Yes | No | Total Number of Respondents |
|---|---|---|---|
| Whites | 27 | 73 | 57 |
| Negroes | 7 | 93 | 170 |

"Do you often get a chance to trade jobs or to fill in on jobs that give you an opportunity to become familiar with work that is different from your own?"

|  | Yes | No | Total Number of Respondents |
|---|---|---|---|
| Whites | 34 | 66 | 57 |
| Negroes | 7 | 93 | 170 |

The network of informal groups at work was described as dividing along racial lines by all but 12 of the 170 unskilled Negro respondents. Only 20 of these respondents reported that they regularly engaged in social activities at work within white groups. There was general agreement among the unskilled Negro workers that there were few instances of regular social contact between Negroes and whites outside the work situation.

The relationship of informal group networks to informal learning opportunities has not been studied extensively, but the emphasis given to them by Negroes in this study suggests the need to research this area carefully.

In this chapter, we have been concerned with some of the attitudes and behaviors of Negro and white workers in companies with equal employment policy and practices. The structure of the samples makes our remarks tentative rather than definitive. Apparently, the majority of these workers had little or no knowledge of the policy or practices. Few of the whites felt that the work environment was discriminatory. Most white workers held that the Negro should be employed according to his abilities. There was strong sentiment among white workers against any company program of preferential treatment for Negroes to equalize opportunities.

It is clear that little intimate social contact existed between Negro and white workers either on the job or outside the plant. There was some exception to this among the most highly trained Negro and white workers--professionals, technicians and administrators.

One of the basic problems among unskilled Negro workers is lack of exposure to informal on-the-job learning processes. Exclusion from informal learning may well act to undermine even the most earnest efforts to employ Negroes. Such exclusion seems to be deeply rooted in the way work is organized in some plants and may be insulated from the attempts of the company to equalize opportunities. It is likely that informal learning and informal sources of job-finding, the latter utilizing present workers to find new workers, may represent highly regarded modes of efficient cost-saving operations to company management and any attempt to make significant changes in these practices will be resisted. This may result in an element of irreducible discrimination that is resistant to pressures from government and civil rights groups.

CHAPTER **6** THE UNION AND EQUAL
EMPLOYMENT OPPORTU-
NITIES IN A COMPANY
SETTING

What is the role of labor unions in the development of an
equal employment program within a company? To what extent do
union policies and practices facilitate or inhibit the equalizing
of opportunities?

The number of unions included in this study is small--eleven
industrial unions and three craft unions. Some information was
obtained on the internationals and state labor councils, but, following our design, primary emphasis was placed on the local unions
and their influence on the development of equal employment opportunities within the company. We are not dealing with a representative sample of unions, but the selected units represent a spectrum
of structures distributed by size, location and variations in membership composition. Data on the selected unions are presented in Table
10.

All but one of the eleven industrial union locals have national
affiliations, whereas two of the three craft unions are so affiliated.
All of the industrial local unions have nondiscrimination clauses
in their contracts; this is not true of any of the three craft unions.
Certainly we are dealing with a select group of industrial local
unions--even the locals in the South have nondiscriminatory clauses--
but this should not be surprising; the companies with which the
unions have contracts are quite select and have taken a firm public
stance in favor of equal employment opportunities.

Interviews were obtained with officers of the fourteen unions.
The presidents of eight industrial local unions and the secretary-
treasurer or vice-president of the other three were interviewed.
The three presidents of the craft unions were interviewed. Wherever
possible, use was made of union memoranda and documents to supply
information required by the schedule.

## UNION-MANAGEMENT COOPERATION
## IN EQUALIZING OPPORTUNITIES

The response patterns in our interviews with corporate executives, local plant personnel and union leaders suggest that the union was a bystander rather than an active participant in company efforts to equalize opportunities. This does not mean that the unions made no effort to improve opportunities for Negroes but that these efforts were largely separate from those of the company. New policy statements on minority group employment were communicated to unions as routine matters; in most cases, the union leaders received information informally about company practices and progress in equalizing opportunities. In the companies studied, bilateral planning and administration of equal employment efforts were not in evidence and apparently were not desired by either union or management. Among management respondents, there was widespread consensus that equalizing employment involved matters of personnel policies and that these were strictly matters of management administration. We have already noted that most management activities in equalizing opportunities primarily emphasized recruitment, a phase of company operations that involved only a few of the craft unions and none of the industrial unions. Union leaders as a group felt that the problem was one that only management could solve because it required changes in personnel matters (e.g., recruitment) over which the union had no control; that involvement in company efforts would compromise the union's position with segments of the white membership; and that the nondiscrimination clause in the contract was the ultimate weapon against inequality of opportunity--nothing further was required.

Viewed in broad perspective, management and union respondents agreed on a number of assumptions regarding equal employment opportunities. First, special efforts must be made, but these should not compromise basic conventions in the company or the union. The company executives felt that these special efforts should not be at the expense of the logic of efficient operation or sound personnel practices already established. Union officials believed that equality of opportunity should not compromise the apprenticeship or seniority system. Second, both groups of respondents believed that the problem was less the responsibility of the company or union and more the responsibility of the Negro himself and the community. Both groups reported there was little that could be done in their respective organizations to solve the problem completely. Finally, both groups viewed the problem in terms of the following factors: inadequate preparation of the Negro for work; negative personal characteristics that made success in work for Negroes doubtful (e.g., lack of ambition); and lack of stable family or community life to support good work habits. There was also general agreement in both groups that race would not stand in the way of Negroes who had adequate skill and training for employment and that there are only a small number of such individuals.

## TABLE 10

## SELECTED CHARACTERISTICS OF FOURTEEN UNION LOCALS

| Union | Member-ship | Location | National affiliation | Nondiscri-minatory clause | Percentage Negro membership |
|---|---|---|---|---|---|
| 1. Industrial, heavy machinery | 4,500 | Large southern city | Yes | Yes | 12 |
| 2. Industrial, steel | 4,000 | Large northern city | Yes | Yes | 63 |
| 3. Industrial, electronics | 800 | Medium southern city | Yes | Yes | 8 |
| 4. Industrial, communications | 3,600 | Large northern city | Yes | Yes | 19 |
| 5. Industrial, electronics | 250 | Small southern city | No | Yes | 4 |
| 6. Industrial, electronics | 1,225 | Medium northern | Yes | Yes | 12 |

| # | Industry | Employees | City | | | |
|---|---|---|---|---|---|---|
| 7. | aerospace | 2,000 | northern city | Yes | Yes | 16 |
| 8. | Industrial, electronics | 1,400 | Medium northern city | Yes | Yes | 16 |
| 9. | Industrial, general manufacturing | 2,300 | Large northern city | Yes | Yes | 17 |
| 10. | Industrial, general manufacturing | 900 | Small southern city | Yes | Yes | 5 |
| 11. | Industrial, general manufacturing | 1,300 | Medium northern city | Yes | Yes | 12 |
| 12. | Craft, transportation | 450 | Small southern city | Yes | No | 5 |
| 13. | Craft, beverage | 1,150 | Large northern city | No | No | 9 |
| 14. | Craft, machinery | 65 | Large northern city | Yes | No | 0 |

It was difficult in all cases of the negotiation of a nondiscrimination clause to determine whether the union or of management had taken the initiative.  Of the twelve companies, data were available for eight.  In five cases, the clauses were inserted at the insistence of union officials after the international union had established such policy.   In the other three cases, the clause was inserted at the request of management.   In three of the first group, the companies with operations in the South strongly objected to the insertion of the clause for fear of alienating white southern workers. The clause was inserted only after protracted negotiations.   In the three cases where management had made the request there was opposition.   One union president admitted that he had wanted the clause for some time but political opposition within the union had restricted his efforts.  The majority of the union leaders felt that initiation of nondiscrimination clauses should ideally be made by the company, since internal union politics frequently inhibited such initiative.

There were some striking differences between the views of leaders of industrial unions and those of craft unions. The following themes occurred time and time again in industrial union interviews:

(1) The union is committed to equalizing opportunities for Negroes.

(2) Little can be done beyond a nondiscrimination clause in the contract.

(3) Equality of opportunity for Negroes should not violate the seniority right of white union members.

(4) The main answer to the problem is to get the Negro to help himself (e.g., more schooling, training).

(5) Future union efforts to help the Negro will involve more training opportunities.

(6) The union leader is restricted in his efforts by the politics of the union and can take limited initiative to help solve the problem.

As a group, industrial union leaders were either sympathetic or passive toward the development of equal job opportunities for the Negro, and, even in the southern-based unions, there was no concerted expression of opposition and hostility toward attempts to equalize opportunities.

In the three craft unions, the response patterns emphasized the following five themes:

(1) Admission to craft union membership should be limited to those Negroes who have the full qualifications, and no preferential treatment should be given. The Negro should be admitted through the same admissions procedures as whites, and authorized union officials should make the determination of admission.

(2) Union membership in the crafts was a "heritage," and union members should have the privilege of recommending relatives and friends as first choices for admission.

(3) Few Negroes have the aptitude or willingness to train to become craft members.

(4) Negroes will gain union admission as soon as more adequate candidates apply.

(5) The main answer to the problem is to get Negroes to help themselves.

The craft union leaders expressed varying degrees of opposition to equalizing opportunities in the craft unions through outside pressure, but were relatively sympathetic to the Negro's integration elsewhere in industry. All three of the craft union respondents felt that their unions were "open to the right Negroes," but admitted that there were strong feelings against Negroes in the union.

These observations would suggest that management-union cooperation in equalizing opportunities hardly exists in these companies either as an ideal or as a practice. However, in industrial unions, there is little expressed opposition to company practices, provided such practices do not appear to compromise the existing job rights of white workers. This may explain why the companies as a group concentrated more on equalizing recruitment and selection opportunities, two areas free of union influence, and paid less attention to training and promotion opportunities, which are subject to some degree of union control through the seniority system.

## COMPANY EXPERIENCES WITH UNIONS IN EQUALIZING OPPORTUNITIES FOR NEGROES

What were the experiences of the companies with the unions during the administration of equal employment practices? What problems arose, and how were they solved? It was a common observation in this study that industrial unions offered little opposition to most equal employment practices of the company. Even in the southern plants, there was less opposition than one would suppose. Several factors may account for this. First, for the most part, company equal employment practices that do not have a direct relevance to union contract provisions are immune from union attack.    Recruitment, hiring and initial placement are considered managerial prerogatives, and there is no open show of opposition to them on the part of most unions.  Second, most industrial unions embrace a democratic ideology, and public expression against Negroes as Negroes would be inappropriate.  Third, it is to the advantage of the union to see employment increase, since most newcomers become dues-paying members.    Finally, a local union that opposes Negro integration can incur government or international union sanctions.

These considerations suggest that union opposition is selective and focuses on situations where job rights of white workers appear threatened.   Opposition to company practices may develop for other issues, but it is the unauthorized wildcat strikers who initiate it, not the union leaders.   There are four company equal employment practices that have invited union opposition:  merging parallel but segregated operations;  eliminating dual seniority lines;  developing merit criteria for training and promotion opportunities;  and eliminating dual lines of progression.

(1) Merging parallel but segregated operations.  It had been company tradition in a large southern plant to operate two parallel but segregated operations.   Action was taken to merge the two operations after a federal compliance review had recommended elimination of this practice.   Union officials strongly objected because some of the white workers would be "bumped" to another job.   A protracted period of negotiation resulted in a decision to merge only part of the operation. Younger Negroes were gradually transferred into the merged operation, but only a handful of the older Negro workers were transferred.

A number of management respondents believed that merging segregated operations arouses the most opposition from unions and inevitably leads to arbitration or mediation.  It was reported that Negroes in another company were unhappy with such a change because their seniority in the merged operation would be reduced to bring them to par with whites.  White union members generally oppose such changes because their seniority standing is reduced and they are frequently "bumped."

(2) Elimination of dual seniority lines.  A widespread practice is to base seniority on departmental rather than plant-wide employment. As a result, Negroes are frequently confined to limited mobility opportunities in low-skill departments (e.g., maintenance), while whites are in departments with greater opportunities.  In one case, whites were permitted to bid across departments; the privilege was denied to Negroes.  Such cases are usually resolved only through long periods of arbitration or mediation.

(3) <u>Merit criteria for training and promotions.</u> In a mid-western plant, the company initiated the practice of considering Negroes for training and promotions based on test profiles. The previous criteria combined experience and seniority. A negotiated settlement with the union permitted limited use of test profiles for the promotion of both whites and Negroes.

(4) <u>Elimination of dual lines of progression.</u> In one of the plants, bidding for jobs in select departments required a certain progression of jobs which most whites had and most Negroes did not. Negotiations brought a settlement that permitted Negroes to bid for certain jobs in these departments even though they were outside the lines of progression.

In many of these instances, the amount of union opposition to the change depends on the following factors. First, what is the status of the practice in nearby plants and in other plants organized by the international union? Frequently, if the practice of segregated operations or work assignments has been eliminated elsewhere, a climate for change develops and union opposition is token. Second, what are the union's expectations in mediation or arbitration? The union leader may engage in arbitration and make only a token show if he has few hopes on the issue. Finally, the climate for acceptance may be far different in an expanding company than in a contracting company.

## CRAFT UNIONS AND EQUAL EMPLOYMENT OPPORTUNITIES

While seniority tends to be a central issue in developing equal employment opportunities in the industrial local union, the apprenticeship issue dominates in the craft unions. The leaders in the three craft unions unanimously observed that resistance to Negroes was based not on skin color but, rather, on the fact that pressures were being exerted to "water down" or eliminate a practice--the apprenticeship system--that craft unionists believed in. These union leaders equated the admission of large numbers of Negroes with the need to compromise or eliminate the apprenticeship system. One of the respondents noted that his union did not discriminate against Negroes per se but, rather, against unqualified Negroes and, in like manner, against unqualified Poles or Germans.

These leaders described three negative consequences of pressures to admit Negroes: standards for apprenticeship would have to be lowered; the traditional father-to-son, or son-surrogate, concept in apprenticeship recruiting would have to be abandoned; and the apprenticeship system would be bypassed as more and more Negroes aspired to journeyman status as a result of training substituted for apprenticeship. The apprenticeship concept was regarded by these leaders as a central issue in admitting the Negro into the crafts.

We have already noted that the stance of the company may be an important consideration in developing equal employment opportunities. The company's attitude may also have an impact on union policies regarding Negro members, even in the South. Thus, in a southern transportation manufacturing center, the Air Force compliance officer took the company to task because there were no Negroes in skilled trade classifications because local union officers who were raised in the South had taken a strong stand against Negro membership in the union. After repeated warnings to the union, the company announced a program of craft training for Negroes in these specialties and guaranteed them jobs in the company after successful completion of the course. When the first two Negroes were placed in jobs, union officials quickly solicited them for membership. Interestingly enough, the apprenticeship system ideal remained intact, for the Negroes were given a three-month period of instruction by journeymen, and this instruction was equated with the apprenticeship training. A similar course of events occurred in a large northern brewery when the management sought to move Negroes into jobs that had previously been "white jobs."

Based on the evidence of this study, industrial union opposition to equal employment practices is not as great as one would believe. If opposition does occur, it is selective and focuses on apparent threats to the job rights of whites. The evidence of this study suggests considerably more opposition in craft unions. Opposition in craft unions is largely centered on the issue of apprenticeship, and attempts to substitute other criteria for admission are strongly opposed. In the development of many equalizing practices, management has little to fear from the industrial unions. Although they may not join and work cooperatively with management to establish an equal employment opportunity program, they do not flatly oppose such a program.

CHAPTER **7** GUIDELINES FOR AFFIRMATIVE ACTION IN EQUAL EMPLOY-MENT OPPORTUNITY

Is it possible to arrive at a set of general principles which can be used as guidelines in the establishment of an affirmative action equal employment program? The term "guidelines" may seem somewhat gratuitous in view of one important finding of this study--such practices are significantly influenced by features unique to the employment situation of any particular firm. However, reference to general principles and to guidelines is justifiable if the following conditions are held in mind.

Viewed at one level, the twenty companies included in this study represent individual case experiences with the development and implementation of affirmative action policies and programs. There are many factors that differentiate these companies--industrial type, unit size, regional location, employment structure and community context. Any discussion of guidelines cannot neglect these various conditions and their ramifications for the content and determination of an equal employment opportunity program.

Less apparent than these obvious differences are common experiences which vary within particular categories of interest (e.g., recruitment, placement, testing) and suggest that general conclusions regarding the structure and programming of equal employment opportunity activities are feasible. The differences noted above should not be allowed to overshadow this fact. No suggestion will be made that any and all such principles are equally applicable to every case; rather, it is our conclusion that these experiences suggest guideposts that can be used to good effect by other employers, many of whom may be taking initial steps toward affirmative action measures.

Those who seek assistance by referring to the experiences of other companies with affirmative action programs should not accept their findings without reservation. Affirmative action is not a unitary term, nor is it one which can be disembodied from the particular circumstances of a company and a community. Techniques and strategies that others have found effective cannot simply be emulated. Because of differences in organizational structures and traditions, modifications are necessary. Affirmative action occurs in many shapes and forms, each of which may be peculiarly effective for a particular set of organizational conditions.

Finally, it has been a central thesis in the study that affirmative action does not result automatically from expressions of good will by company executives or from the issuance of a public policy statement. Although these are vital, a realistic and positive appraisal of the company's potential is the necessary ingredient. Careful assessment and programming can spell the difference between success and disillusionment.

In deriving general guidelines for affirmative action, we have not shied away from drawing upon the findings of other studies concerned with the equalization of employment opportunity in American industry. In one sense, this discussion reflects the cumulative experiences of many researchers and practitioners who have examined the problems, promises, fads and foibles of affirmative action programs. By dividing our discussion according to categories, we express our concern that an affirmative action program be viewed as multifaceted and touching upon all parts of the employment process, though perhaps not with equal degrees of emphasis.

## FORMULATION OF AN EQUAL EMPLOYMENT OPPORTUNITY POLICY

Careful consideration must be given to the formulation of an equal employment opportunity policy. Rightly considered, this policy will (or should) provide the basic direction for the development of operating procedures to implement the affirmative action program. It represents a company commitment of major dimensions.

Two immediate considerations affect the formulation of an affirmative action policy. First, it is true that many companies have had an explicit or implicit nondiscrimination policy for many years. Thus, the development of an affirmative action program may be viewed not as a new policy, but as a continuation of an already existing one, with the new emphases reaffirming or clarifying management's commitment to equal employment opportunity objectives. However this may be, experiences have shown that no assumption should be made that a pre-existing policy statement is an adequate foundation for new emphases. Affirmative action does not just happen; objectives and operating procedures must be carefully thought out.

Second, companies vary in the degree of formality involved in the establishment of general employment policies. Some officials in companies that tend toward the informal pattern regard as moot the question whether the formulation of an equal employment opportunity policy should depart radically from usual procedures.

In either case, there is little question that the company's top management needs to state clearly its affirmative action commitment in policy form. A relevant distinction in this respect can be made between policy statements and policy decisions. Policy statements serve a public relations function. The latter represent commitments of company resources to policy implementation. Policy decisions should clarify objectives and mandate an aggressive campaign for their achievement. The distinction is a viable one in that, while company tradition may not favor a written policy statement, there can be little question of the necessity of a policy decision.

Policy decisions should serve three basic purposes: express the company's commitment to the goal of equal employment opportunity; reflect realistic but definite targets to be achieved; and emphasize the company's intentions in the minds of the managers and supervisors who will be responsible for the operating program.

The following principles are generally applicable in the formulation of an equal employment policy:

(1) The policy should be developed with the full backing of top officials in the company, including the chief officer. This backing must not be merely symbolic. Key executives should be involved both in formulating the basic policy and in establishing the operating procedures for its implementation.

(2) The equal employment policy should reflect an adequate appraisal of the company's potential for expanding minority group employment opportunities. Platitudinous statements are less important than a clear statement of objectives that are within the company's reach. Some companies will be employing their first Negro workers; others may have had Negro employees for a number of years in lower-level jobs. The formulation of policy should consider both the company's present circumstance and its potential for change.

(3) The policy should be formulated in such a manner that it is recognized as a major policy commitment, rather than a low priority administrative item.

(4) An affirmative action program touches many, if not all, parts of the employment structure of a company, and there should be no doubt about the policy's application to all of these--hiring, placement, supervision, training, upgrading and promotion.

## COMMUNICATION OF POLICY

There is a subtle distinction in terms that can be introduced to good effect. "Communicating the policy" and "announcing the policy" are not fully synonymous. The former encompasses the latter but contains much more. Here, we are primarily concerned with the more limited term, but it should be recognized that the communication of an equal employment policy is accomplished as much by actions as by public pronouncements. The time-worn phrase, "Action speaks louder than words," is well borne out in the experiences of those who have formulated and operated affirmative action programs. In fact, Negro and white workers and community members are often skeptical and suspicious that the policy may not be a firm commitment, and their reactions are not simply dispelled by paper communications.

None of the above should be construed as depreciating the importance of disseminating information about the equal employment policy. There is general agreement, however, that these communications should be carefully planned and controlled. In general, they should be targeted only to those persons and agencies which in some manner affect the policy's operation or control the flow of manpower to the company. An uncontrolled communication pattern, particularly with respect to organizations and media outside the company, could possibly be detrimental in that it may be viewed as a public relations gesture rather than a sincere commitment or it may result in job applications by minority group members who, in numbers and/or qualifications, cannot be accepted for employment. Many recommend that these media be used only when significant accomplishments in equal opportunity have been made.

The strategies decided upon for communicating the policy ultimately depend upon company traditions and managerial styles. However, there are two key questions involved in the process of communication:    To whom should the policy be communicated, and what are the most effective means of communication? Neither can be answered by statements applicable to all situations, but the observations offered below incorporate suggestions that emerge from the experiences of many employers.

## Communication Within the Company

The general suggestion is that personnel at all levels within the company should be informed of the policy and that all such announcements should carry the stamp of top management approval. This does not imply that the content and depth of information should be the same throughout or that the same announcement is made to all at the same time. Most experienced employers advise the provision of advance information for supervisory personnel, the rationale being that this enables those who will directly administer the policy to act with confidence and authority. Nonsupervisory employees should also be made aware of the policy, although there is some disagreement as to how this is best effected. In most cases, a combination of formal and informal means have been used to disseminate information about the policy within a company.

A point not often made, but one that can be of significance in some communities, is communication of the company's nondiscrimination policy to job applicants when they appear at the employment office. Of course, this may already have been accomplished by the appending of an "Equal Opportunity Employer" notice in "help wanted" ads, or by signs appropriately placed in the employment office itself. But the inclusion of a statement about the company's stance on equal employment opportunity at the time of processing the job application can assure that the company's position is understood by prospective employees.

Many employers recommend that procedures established to process grievances concerning discrimination should be specified when the policy is announced. This type of action may serve two purposes. It can again reflect management's commitment to an equal employment opportunity program as a reality rather than merely as an idea; and it may forestall the possibility of incidents arising from interracial friction moving outside the company gates and becoming "community incidents."

## Communication of Policy to the Union

Most company executives who have engaged in the initial formulation and communication of an equal employment policy agree that announcement to unions with which the company has collective bargaining agreements should be a simple and forthright statement of objectives. Some contend that even this is unnecessary, for such a policy is solely a managerial responsibility.

However this question is resolved, one point is fairly clear. It is quite possible that an affirmative action program may necessitate some modifications of practices that are relevant to union-management agreements. These are matters of negotiation; primary concern, at this point, is with the communication of a policy that, in effect, is unilaterally determined. The basic purpose of this communication, if attempted at all, is to solicit union support and cooperation.

## Communication of Policy to Employment Agencies and Other Sources of Manpower Supply

There are two points of reference for the guidelines here. On one hand, there are sources of recruitment that a company may be regularly using (e.g., public and private employment agencies, vocational training schools, community high schools, colleges and universities); these should be informed of the policy. In addition, the nature of an equal employment opportunity policy itself mandates the early establishment of contacts with possible new sources of recruitment (e.g., predominantly Negro high schools and colleges; Negro civic agencies).

In all the above cases, it should be emphasized that communicating the company's equal employment policy is an important component of affirmative action, but it is only an initial step. These employers with experience concur in their judgment that such announcements by themselves produce few minority group job applicants. As stated previously, an equal employment policy is only a statement of intent until basic decisions are made to commit company resources to its implementation. Until this is done, it is only an imaginary program which will yield--as experience clearly shows--imaginary results.

What are the most effective techniques for communicating the equal employment opportunity policy? The answer to this will vary according to availability of means, size of company and, not of least importance, managerial ingenuity. Some of the techniques that have been used to good effect, often in combination, are:

(1) Orientation sessions with managerial and supervisory personnel. These meetings can fulfill several purposes. They convey the message that top management considers the policy to be of major importance and is unequivocal in its commitment. They provide an opportunity for lower-echelon managers and supervisors to  raise pertinent questions about operating procedures, thus avoiding ambiguity and uncertainty about responsibilities. They offer an opportunity to determine specific implications of the general guidelines typically established in policy formulations. In companies of considerable size, they can provide assurance that information about the policy is uniformly disseminated in all units and every supervisor is informed of his responsibilities under the program.

(2) A statement to the work group by the supervisor. Some recommend this strategy on the assumption that the immediate supervisor is in the best position to anticipate and deal with workers' reactions.

(3) A letter signed by the president or a vice-president and sent to every employee. This has one advantage in that it expresses the commitment of the chief officer or other top executive.

(4) A letter to managerial and supervisory personnel with copies posted on bulletin boards.

(5) Notices of the policy placed on bulletin boards only.

(6) Inclusion of the policy statement in employee handbooks.

(7) Statements in memoranda, following the usual channels of transmittal.

(8) Statement and discussion of the equal employment policy in supervisors' handbooks.

(9) Articles regarding the policy (and particularly achievements) in company publications.

(10) Special publications explaining the policy and the program's objectives.

(11) Contacts through letters and individual visits by company representatives to outside agencies and groups to explain the company's policy and objectives.

Whatever methods are chosen to communicate the equal employment opportunity policy, past experiences suggest a general precaution--the content of the communication should be forceful but forthright and not convey an impression to present employees or others that the company is relaxing its standards of job qualification or performance.

## ADMINISTRATION OF NONDISCRIMINATION EMPLOYMENT PRACTICES

The administration of an affirmative action policy incorporates two interdependent but distinguishable dimensions. On one hand, practices must be established to deal with specific components of the employment structure. On the other hand, the operating policy should be administratively organized and controlled in order to assure continuity of effort as well as feedback of information about progress and suggested modifications. At this point, attention is focused on the latter.

How the administrative system for organizing and controlling affirmative action practices is established depends on several factors. As the brief case descriptions given in Chapter 4 imply, the existing corporate structure tends to set limits on feasible administrative practices and control procedures. In some cases, administrative control is highly centralized, with little delegation of decision-making authority to operating units. In others, there is a strong tradition of decentralization and much delegation of administrative responsibility. The combined experiences of many employers suggest that affirmative action programs are most effective when they do not radically depart from established procedures of administrative control. This suggests that no single blueprint can be applicable to all companies.

The preceding point should not be construed as implying that administrative innovation is unnecessary for the development of an effective equal employment opportunity program. It may well be the case, particularly in companies that have had implicit or explicit nondiscrimination policies for many years, that a key problem to be  faced will be inertia within the present system. But innovation does not necessarily mean upheaval. Working on the assumption that the adoption of an equal employment policy does require some form of innovative activity, the following points may be instructive before moving on to more specific considerations of administrative control. Administrative innovation may utilize one or another of the following modes for introducing change into the organization: establishing a new unit within the corporate structure, charged with primary responsibilities for implementing the new policy; interpolating new functions into existing corporate structure, thus improvising but not basically altering; and continuing with existing arrangements, under the assumption that no new inputs are necessary to bring about a desired state of affairs.

What are the arguments pro and con for each of the above three points? First of all, at a practical level, it can be pointed out that the first pattern (establishing a new unit) is seldom found in companies that have developed equal employment opportunity policies. Only two instances of this were discovered in the present study, and, in both cases, the companies were of major size and had highly formalized and complex administrative structures. Each company previously used this procedure to introduce new programs that represented a major policy commitment. It is important to note, however, that in neither case were the administrative responsibilities for the equal employment policy completely isolated within the new unit. Rather, the delegated responsibilities were in the direction of coordination, performance review and information feedback to other operating units.

Others have argued that the creation of new units, besides being costly and time-consuming, overestimates the innovative character of an equal employment opportunity program. The rationale underlying this argument is that, while in the initial stages there may be "crash efforts" to get the program moving, the ultimate goal should be to incorporate equal employment objectives into general employment procedures. Thus, the creation of a new unit may give the impression that an equal employment program is distinct from the company's general practices. In addition, the argument is made that most phases of affirmative action must ultimately be carried out by operating units at all organizational levels; disengaging control from these units may make it operationally inconclusive.

More commonly found are administrative procedures of the second type (the interpolation of new functions into existing units), although concrete examples extend across a wide range of possibilities. Some conditioning factors are company size, geographical concentration or dispersion of installations and degree of formalization and complexity of administrative structure. Typically, responsibilities for program coordination and storage of information relevant to minority group employment are lodged within a particular unit, but operating assignments are widely spread throughout the organization. The unit may also act as a central point for dealing with problems that arise occasionally but not continually (e.g., grievance and discipline problems that cannot be easily handled at their points of origin).

Arguments favoring this type of administrative organization point to its flexibility. Resources are definitely committed to an affirmative action program, but additional resources can be mobilized to meet needs and problems that often arise but are difficult to predict in advance. As relative emphases on program components shift over time (e.g., initial recruitment to training and upgrading), expertise relevant to specific issues can be brought to bear.

The third alternative neither changes structure nor extends functions. The implicit assumptions are that existing arrangements are adequate and that a simple statement of policy can stimulate movement toward implementation. But results may be disappointing, and most employers have found this strategy to be unsatisfactory in providing tangible evidence of affirmative action.

As noted previously, whichever general model is followed will depend partly on the company's capabilities as well as managerial style and level of commitment to affirmative action objectives. There are, however, several individual components of administration that must be considered under any circumstance, and these are treated below.

Creating an Administrative Structure for Affirmative Action

The cumulative experiences of employers who have formulated equal employment opportunity policies indicate that giving attention to the administration of affirmative action programs pays dividends in that it clearly demonstrates management's commitment, removes ambiguity about responsibilities under the policy, and goes far in assuring a coordinated company effort.

In this section, we shall discuss four important features of the administrative structure underlying affirmative action. We wish to emphasize again that no single pattern can be adopted without modifications that take into account unique company situations. To date, most of the pressures for affirmative action have been directed toward business firms of comparatively large size, and, thus, much of our current knowledge about equal employment opportunity policies is dependent on reported experience of fairly large employers. Demands for affirmative action are becoming more widespread and are affecting many companies with smaller, informal and less complex employment operations.

The preferred method of instituting affirmation action, as discussed in the preceding section, will partially dictate administrative needs. The extent of employer commitment and employer capability for engaging in affirmative action are contingencies which condition the actual operating program.

## Assignment of Administrative Responsibilities

Earlier, it was stated that affirmative action doesn't "just happen." It is the result of policy commitment, purposeful administrative practice and the assignment of administrative responsibility to carry through policy implementation.

The assignment of responsibilities for policy implementation should be made with the assurance that the implications of the policy are known and understood at all operating levels. How this is best accomplished depends upon several factors. As noted earlier, a few large companies decided to create a new administrative unit to coordinate and oversee affirmative action practices. Others have chosen to extend the functions of already existing units to include administrative responsibilities to carry through the equal employment opportunity policy. Our evidence indicates that, for the most part, in companies using the second pattern, the responsibility is typically located within the personnel, industrial relations or employee relations department, with the reporting system extending upwards to at least the vice-presidential level. It is true that some employers prefer not to program assignments of personnel, but to allow the policy to act as its own stimulus. Our observations disclose that the ratio of success is lowest when this alternative is chosen. In any event, the policy decision regarding equal employment opportunity should incorporate some guidelines concerning its administration. Company size is also a variable that cannot be ignored. Generally speaking, large companies have more complex administrative structures, and, while this may afford opportunities for more definitive programming of responsibilities, it also may mandate a more formal statement of objectives. This may be particularly true in the case of corporations with central offices and local installations geographically dispersed. How the policy, as formulated at corporate headquarters, becomes translated into action at the local, or operating, level depends upon the degree of equivalence in policy interpretation between company officials at each end. Assigning definite responsibilities for coordinating and clarifying policy objectives can provide insurance against misinterpretation and delays in action.

Smaller companies with simpler and more informal administrative structures have some advantages in that administrative offices are usually more consolidated and lines of communication are shorter. But there are possible pitfalls. The simpler and more informal pattern may lead to an unwarranted assumption that objectives and responsibilities are more clearly understood than they actually are. This is a danger to be guarded against.

Although certain practices relating to affirmative action (e.g., coordination, performance review) may be centralized within a particular company unit, it is necessary for all managers and supervisors to share responsibilities for policy implementation. In most companies, a division of operating responsibilities will be clearly indicated. For example, line departments may be much closer to points of hiring and upgrading, whereas personnel or industrial relations officials may have greater expertise in recruitment. In one sense, this is another way of saying that success necessitates the incorporation of affirmative action practices into the general employment structure, even in those instances where a unit is newly created to oversee the equal employment opportunity policy. Assignment of responsibilities and coordination of efforts are the keynotes.

## Allocating Resources for Affirmative Action

To be effective, an equal employment policy demands allocation of company resources for its implementation. Many employers can testify that the simple statement of an equal employment policy is a sterile gesture that may lead to little, if any, results. Any or all of the following activities may be necessary: establishment of contacts with new sources of recruitment; review of current minority group employees, with a view to upgrading where possible; careful cultivation of community sentiments; review and possible modification of selection and testing procedures; re-examination of company-sponsored social activities; and desegregation of company facilities. None of these are accomplished without the investment of time, staff and resources.

## Establishing a System for Control and Audit

What are the specific aspects of the administrative arrangements that need to be established for policy implementation? Many a well-intentioned employer has been disappointed by the meager results of affirmative action in his company. Besides the patterning of administrative responsibilities and the provision of resources, there must also be processes of control and auditing as inventories of progress. Of course, this is more easily said than done. A review of the three case examples discussed in Chapter 4 clearly illustrates that existing corporate structure will place limits upon the control and auditing pattern followed.

In some cases, control can be very direct, although informal. This is best demonstrated by companies in which administrative control is not highly formalized and policy decisions by executive fiat are the rule rather than the exception. In companies with highly formalized, bureaucratic structures, control may be less direct but nonetheless effective. In companies with highly decentralized patterns of administration, with great autonomy lodged in operating management, effective control, whether direct or indirect, is difficult to achieve. In this case, except for internal modification of employment structure or pressures applied directly to operating units, a control and audit system will be virtually impossible to develop.

In the present study, we found many concrete illustrations of policy control, extending from highly formalized paper systems to the very informal (e.g., personal visits or telephone calls to local managers or department heads), from the very coercive to the gently persuasive. But whether formal or informal, direct or indirect, in all companies that demonstrated some degree of effectiveness in affirmative action, identifiable patterns of control and auditing procedures were in evidence. In these companies, no assumptions were made that affirmative action practices would be self-starting.

### Evaluating the Effectiveness of Affirmative Action Practices

Effectiveness in affirmative action can be measured by employment statistics, useful indicators of progress or lack of progress. Every company included in the present study utilized some statistical reporting system of employment data. Most of the companies were reporting these data either as government contractors, as members of Plans for Progress, or on request from a local or state agency. It can be taken as axiomatic that a program of affirmative action must include a periodic inventory of employees by race. In large corporations, the reporting system may be quite formal, with field reports submitted on a scheduled basis. In smaller firms, procedures may be less formal, even to the extent of reliance on personal observation by key officials. In any event, systematic collection of employment data must be instituted as a check on progress. These data should contain, where possible, employment statistics by occupational level and data on promotion and upgrading.

While there is little question of the need for employment statistics as baseline data, a more important question concerns the use to which these data are put. If, as is true in some cases, operating units send reports up the line to a staff office, which acts only to store and/or transmit the data to an outside agency, use of reports as self-corrective tools is virtually nil. Experience has shown that reports can be used to good effect within the company provided that the company's commitment to equal employment opportunity is firm and an administrative pattern for policy implementation has been established. Some of the functions fulfilled by audit systems are the following: to provide for feedback of information to reporting units and to provide such units with a survey analysis of progress or lack of progress; to provide a basis for further discussion about the policy with a view to finding out what has produced results and what has not; and to provide suggestions for additional work at weak points (e.g., a step-up in recruitment efforts).

Admittedly, record-keeping is a chore, and one that many would prefer to avoid. Nonetheless, apart from periodic inventory of employment, there is virtually no way to gauge the current situation or measure progress. In the preceding discussion, continuity of effort was emphasized as a key feature of affirmative action. The accumulation and feedback of information about minority group employment is a basic requisite for this process.

## AFFIRMATIVE ACTION AND THE EMPLOYMENT STRUCTURE

The preceding discussion has emphasized the need for effective administrative control and direction of affirmative action practices. In this section, several components of the employment structure are examined for their relationship to equal employment opportunities. Major emphasis is placed on recruitment procedures. The discussion proceeds on the assumption that affirmative action may require the addition of new employment practices, the extension or modification of others or even the elimination of some.

### Recruitment

Recruitment is widely regarded as the most important component of affirmative action. An active recruitment effort generally involves two major approaches: a re-examination of current recruiting practices to see if they inadvertently discriminate against minority group job applicants; and the establishment of contacts with new sources of manpower supply, particularly within the minority group community. Each of these is discussed below from the standpoint of some specific strategies and techniques which employers have found effective:

(1) Current patterns of recruitment may be directly or indirectly discriminatory. This can occur, for example, when a company has come to depend heavily upon referrals from present employees. If the current work force is largely or completely composed of white employees, continued reliance on personal referrals can perpetuate the exclusion of minority group members. Even in cases where minority group members are already employed by the company, if they are concentrated in unskilled jobs, personal referrals will generally produce few qualified minority group applicants for higher-skilled jobs.

(2) Typically, companies come to rely on a few outside agencies for referral of applicants. In many cases these are private and public employment agencies that, in the past, may not have been

productive sources for minority group referrals. This does not imply that they cannot be, and each should be clearly advised of the company's equal employment policy and affirmative action objectives.

(3) Contacts must also be established with special sources of recruitment that can assist in supplying referrals of minority group job applicants. In the early stages of an affirmative action program, it is advisable to place considerable emphasis on the cultivation of such contacts. How extensive these efforts should or can be is affected by a number of company conditions. First, the manpower needs of the company, particularly with reference to the skill levels for which recruits are sought, will partially determine the character of the recruiting program. Larger companies are increasingly placing greater emphasis on finding Negroes with professional and technical skills. This is commendable, but the search for individuals qualified for lesser-skilled entry level jobs should not be neglected. Nor should the possibility of upgrading present Negro employees be overlooked. Second, special recruitment efforts will be affected by the network of professional leaders and civic agencies available within the local minority group community. Third, the resources that can be allocated to special recruiting activities will vary from company to company. Larger companies have some over-all advantage in that corporate staff and local staff can coordinate their efforts, thus making the "talent search" national, regional and/or local.

Special recruiting procedures for affirmative action can incorporate a wide range of types, extending from the very indirect and impersonal to the very direct and personal. Some examples of indirect and impersonal procedures include the addition of an "Equal Opportunity Employer" slogan to advertisements in newspapers and other public media; sponsorship of employment advertisements in journals or other publications catering to Negro or other minority group subscribers; and dissemination of information about the company's policy via company publications or trade journals. Many employers who have operated affirmative action programs feel that these techniques are useful and necessary but effective only when used to complement more direct and personal contacts.

More direct or personal contacts are those that link the company to individuals and associations in touch with potential job applicants. There are many examples of these. Some companies encourage their executives to serve on commissions, special committees and boards of agencies that deal with minority group problems. Such civic activities have value, although they are no substitute for direct recruiting. Some companies engage in the sponsorship or cosponsorship of community programs and activities that are directly linked to the recruitment of minority group workers. These programs may be short- or long-range in perspective. Examples include participation in high school "career day" programs;

conducting students, teachers and counselors on tours of company facilities; participation in work experience programs after school hours; and participation in job orientation and placement programs conducted by such agencies as the Urban League. Some companies request referrals from minority group organizations, such as Negro civic agencies and churches, or from minority group community leaders. Experienced employers recommend that the company's manpower needs and its selection standards be fully clarified to the individuals and organizations approached. Neglecting this may cause embarrassment and possibly antagonism. It should also be recognized that such persons and organizations are usually besieged with requests for referrals from employers. Singular reliance on this type of contact may prove disappointing. Requests for referrals from vocational and educational guidance agencies may prove valuable, particularly with respect to agencies with significant numbers of minority group clients. Recruitment at high schools, training schools and colleges with significant numbers of minority group members in the student body is a fairly standard strategy. Most experienced employers recommend working directly with placement officers in order to acquaint them with the firm's employment needs.

### Other Components of Employment Structure
### and Affirmative Action

For employers who have employed few or no minority group workers in the past, recruitment is the sine qua non of affirmative action. Certainly, our most complete information about equal employment opportunity practices concerns recruitment strategies and techniques for increasing minority group employment. It is probable that most employers enjoy greater latitude for innovation and experimentation in matters of recruitment than in any other aspect of the employment process. But establishing an equal employment policy must not end with recruitment. To be effective, affirmative action must pervade the company's entire employment structure.

In this section, other components of the company's employment procedures that affect and are affected by affirmative action practices will be treated. The discussion will be brief and confined to major issues and questions that must be faced. Several points that could have been included here have been thoroughly discussed in earlier chapters, and, therefore, will not be reviewed here.

In the current study, employers generally concurred that affirmative action that deviates from established employment standards is self-defeating. The generally accepted principle seems to be that all phases of employment should be administered equitably, with individuals judged only by criteria that are job-related. In sum, this is the meaning assigned to the term "equal employment opportunity." But the actual working out of the principle depends on the word "equitably." How it is defined and put into practice? What are some of the issues involved in assuring that all phases of employment are administered equitably?

There is considerable variation among companies as to the specific procedures used in accepting or rejecting job applicants. Many companies use combinations of personal interviews, aptitude and personality tests, records of past employment experiences and personal references. Others rely mainly on the personal interview, typically informal in nature, with the evaluation of qualifications depending heavily on subjective impressions.

Whether formal or informal, complex or simple, selection procedures incorporate a series of reference points used in making decisions to accept or reject job applicants. Frequently, the specific techniques are products of tradition or convenience, and few attempts have been made to validate results as predictors of performance on the job. This is particularly true when the tests used have been standardized on national samples. The important criterion for any technique is whether it is a valid predictor of job performance in the local situation.

The basic purpose of selection standards is objectivity in evaluation of qualifications and elimination of considerations that are unrelated to job performance. A new look at selection and testing procedures is an important component of affirmative action. This should include frequent re-examination of testing procedures; an appraisal of employment prerequisites to see if the standards are realistic and necessary; and a check on those who make hiring decisions to make certain that all applicants are equitably considered.

Few of the respondents in the present study considered job placement to be a major issue in minority group employment. Some did admit, however, to exercising caution when the "first" Negro was placed on the job, assuming that a successful pilot experience contributed to later favorable results. More frequently, the contention was that management's firmness and determination to see that the equal employment policy was actively pursued proved to be the most important ingredient of success. Available evidence suggests that anticipations of employee resistance to the policy tend to be exaggerated, and weaknesses occur when management equivocates in its policy commitment or is administratively incapable of demanding compliance at operating levels.

Promotion and upgrading are important features of affirmative action practices. However, it is true that a company's capability in providing opportunities to minority group employees for promotion or upgrading may be limited by several conditions. Turnover rates may be low within a company, and, thus, few job openings will occur. In addition, procedures for promotion and upgrading may be partially determined by company-union contract agreements, particularly in cases where lines of progression and seniority rights in job bidding are rigidly determined. Some companies, however, are not so restricted and can be more flexible with respect to promotion and upgrading opportunities. No single pattern for affirmative action can be recommended, but the following techniques have been used to provide greater opportunities for minority group employees. First, some companies have instituted reviews of the personnel files of current minority group employees to see if some may qualify as candidates for higher-level jobs. This has proved to be particularly effective in cases where, because of local tradition, individuals may have been reticent to come forward on their own. Second, re-examination of the seniority system and lines of job progression may disclose that minority group employees are "frozen" in certain departments and excluded from equitable consideration for promotion and upgrading. Third, in companies where promotion procedures are not formally prescribed, policies and practices should be periodically reviewed and audited to insure impartiality.

Opportunities for training are important features of affirmative action in that training is often a requisite for job mobility. Much training in American industry is of an informal, on-the-job type, although two other types are frequently found: tuition-relief programs for employees who attend classes at some outside training installation, and apprenticeship training programs which are usually associated with preparation for entry into the skilled crafts. Affirmative action with respect to training opportunities should be twofold. The equal employment policy should be administratively controlled so that qualified minority group employees are included in training programs; and minority group employees should be actively encouraged to increase their skills and job potential through participation in available training and educational programs. The latter may necessitate counseling efforts expressly undertaken for this purpose.

Needless to say, the existence of segregated company facilities or company sponsorship of segregated social activities for employees gives the lie to policy pronouncements. The experiences of many employers who have faced one or the other, or both, of these problems, suggest that they are best eliminated with as little fanfare as possible.

In this section, no attempt has been made to cover the gamut of possibilities and problems of affirmative action. Many suggestions can be gleaned from discussions in previous chapters. These points are clear, however:

(1) Affirmative action touches upon all phases of employment within a company. Although recruiting processes are key features of affirmative action, the equal employment opportunity policy should be defined as covering all components of the employment structure.

(2) Specific techniques of affirmative action will be effective only insofar as they are backed up and coordinated through a clear assignment of administrative responsibilities and program-auditing procedures. Inertia is, typically, the greatest obstacle to affirmative action.

CHAPTER **8** RESEARCH AND POLICY
IMPLICATIONS OF
THE STUDY


Equal employment opportunities for Negroes is a subject that is beset by complexity and by emotions. Any statement on the subject is bound to be challenged by one, or all, of the following interested parties: corporate decision-makers; union leaders; civil rights leaders; government policy-makers; or rank-and-file Negro and white workers. Nevertheless, it is fitting to conclude with some thoughts on the development of equal employment opportunities for Negro workers.

It must be reasserted that this study was not an attempt to survey exhaustively the problems of equal employment opportunities for Negro workers in the country. The following remarks shall necessarily be circumscribed by the observations and insights gathered from a very select group of companies, their unions, and their white and Negro workers. The purpose was to uncover some of the basic factors that perpetuated or reduced discrimination against Negroes in twenty companies--and not to discover the "cause" of all employment inequality that Negroes experience. Such remarks must necessarily involve suggestions and recommendations for social policy in this field, as well as suggestions for further research.


## POLICY RECOMMENDATIONS


One of the key problems in implementing an equal employment opportunity program is to find a suitable basis for an intensive effort by management. This study suggests that the effort, if it does come, will be within the framework of existing company employment practices. In a free enterprise system, the expectation is that voluntary action will suffice to equalize opportunities, but the experience in the 1960's has shown that such action must be complemented with persuasive forces from the outside to result in extensive change. Contract compliance machinery, for example, has now been in evidence for some time and has made a valuable contribution in developing effective equal employment opportunity practices in many companies.

In a broad sense, the equalizing of employment opportunities for Negroes requires the concerted and cooperative action of a number of institutions in our society: business, labor, government and education. It is within this framework that the following specific policy recommendations are made.

## Implications of the Study

The observations on the twenty companies suggest a number of practices that might facilitate the recruitment, hiring and up-grading of Negroes in American industry. Nine of these practices deserve to be emphasized:

(1) The principle of "outreach." It is clear that the recruit-ment of Negro workers, particularly those with skill, requires some degree of "outreach." Negro workers do not respond auto-matically when the hiring sign is out. Most companies in this study found it necessary to go to the Negro neighborhood, the Negro school or the Negro church to recruit. However crude these attempts were, recruitment was facilitated by such activities.

The spatial and social ghettoization of the Negro makes it difficult for the company to gain direct access to the Negro worker through normal channels of recruitment. Successful recruitment requires the building of links between industry and the Negro com-munity--its citizens and institutions. In early recruitment, the company must establish some roots in the Negro community. In some cases, there may be a company field office; more fre-quently, there is systematic support for Negro agencies and organi-zations (e.g., the Urban League). The principle of "outreach" suggests, then, not only company recruiting in the Negro community but the sustained support of Negro organizations and structures that attempt to ameliorate Negro work problems.

Besides being practiced by the company, the principle of "outreach" must be adopted by all agencies, public and private, that are involved in the manpower process. The state employment service, the vocational school, job clinics--these do little good if they are not physically and psychologically based in the Negro community. The detached social worker who makes himself at home with the gang on the street should have a parallel in the manpower agencies if their prevocational services are to have an effect.

(2) The need for job development.  The observations of the
minority group practices in these companies suggest that special
efforts must be made to fit Negro workers into the work force.
Special efforts may be minimal for skilled workers, but, in the
case of nonskilled workers, the company and community agencies
must engage in special job development.  This may involve either
providing the worker with special job preparation--before or during
employment--or changing the work requirements to make the
Negro eligible for employment.  In both cases, more than simple
job placement is required.  There may be the need to provide the
worker with special social skills for the job, a more satisfactory
transportation arrangement or special tools and medical treatment.
Extensive follow-up services (psychological, medical or vocational)
may be required for an extensive period after he enters the job
situation.    In any case, there is a continuous need to sift and
examine the demands of the job and the worker's needs in adapting
to them.    It is a serious mistake to feel that the job is complete
when the Negro is recruited and hired.  Usually, much remains
to be done during the period of employment.

(3) The need for job creation.  The equalizing of opportunities
may demand a total review of the employment structure and the
creation of new jobs.    Employers in this study frequently found
that when Negro workers could not qualify for job openings, some
amelioration was possible by creating new jobs in which the worker
could perform productively and enlarge his skills to qualify for a
"regular" job.    This strategy usually helped both employer and
worker--the former by filling a portion of his manpower needs
and the latter by providing work experience in a setting where job
promotion or enlargement was possible.

(4) The need to review testing and interviewing procedures.
Frequently, discrimination is unintentional, resulting from the per-
petuation of traditional or outdated interviewing or testing procedures
that eliminate many job applicants from consideration.    It was a
frequent experience that a re-examination of these practices and
particularly their role in placement and promotion opportunities
resulted in modification of job entry requirements.

(5) The need to establish special procedures in upgrading or
promotions.    Only a small number of the companies had established
special aids in upgrading or promotions, and these were companies
in high-growth industries (electronics, heavy manufacturing).  Two
essential elements were present in these cases: systematic review
of worker job histories and special counseling programs to advise
workers of new job openings or chances for advancement.

(6) The need for job rotation to increase opportunities for
informal learning on the job.  It was obvious from this study that
Negroes are seriously disadvantaged in informal work-learning
opportunities.    The Negro may be locked into a job because he has

had no access to informal learning situations that pave the way for job mobility. The employer must develop mechanisms either through collective bargaining or changes in employment policy to insure rotation of jobs and equal access to informal learning.

(7) The need to enlarge traditional meanings of affirmative action. It was obvious in this study that few companies viewed the affirmative action principle as an evolving concept, needing to be redefined as new minority group employment problems are approached. The affirmative action principle must necessarily evolve from the strict application of nondiscriminatory standards in employment policy (i.e., only job-related characteristics are relevant) to a stage where "outreach" procedures are added to encourage the recruitment of minority group applicants. But this is not enough. In time, true affirmative action must include preferential or compensatory employment practices to give jobs to the hard-to-employ minority group member. These latter efforts to compensate the Negro for past inequalities poses a dilemma for most companies, for they are being asked to employ workers who may not initially meet existing standards of production. Frequently, the company can obtain help in such a program from a number of sources: on-the-job training subsidies from government funds and supportive counseling and training services from public and private agencies. A necessary principle of operation for companies in such a program is to inventory and utilize manpower services offered by public and private agencies in the community.

(8) The need to consider the broader context of minority group employment problems. In this study, the companies that had made gains in equalizing employment opportunities were the companies that had examined minority group employment problems in a broader context than merely equalizing opportunities in the company. The development of sound equal employment policy operations within a company requires an awareness of community manpower trends as well as of industry and national trends in employment. In the last analysis, the integration of Negroes into American industry is an employment rather than a moral issue. Effective planning demands a knowledge of Negro capabilities and existing patterns of utilization in the labor force. A company must become aware of the institutional barriers within his community and industry that contribute to the misuse of Negro resources. In this respect, there is no substitute for ongoing research and record-keeping to pinpoint barriers as well as to measure progress. As analyses of EEO-1 forms become available, this information can be used to expand the information resources of the company.

(9) The need for constant review of changing technological and personnel needs in the company. Most companies as a matter of course develop statistics on technological change and emerging personnel needs. All of the companies in the study gathered statistics on employment by race, but few kept records on job

applicants by race. It was obvious that, in companies with marked success in equalizing employment, some attempt had been made to collate data from minority group employment forms with emerging technological and personnel patterns. On the other hand, companies with less successful programs viewed each of these two sets of data independently.

In summary, then, our data indicate the need for very specific actions to enlarge job opportunities for Negroes. In most cases, the doors had opened or were opening. The recruitment of Negroes who qualified for jobs under existing standards was becoming more difficult, and there was increasing pressure to use energies and resources to improve the quality of the minority group labor market.

## RESEARCH RECOMMENDATIONS

The research recommendations incorporate the insights gained in the present study as well as the author's growing acquaintance with research needs in the field. Eight specific recommendations will be discussed in order of priority:

(1) A central facility should be established under either university, foundation or government sponsorship to function as a clearinghouse for equal employment studies in companies and communities. Such a facility should be something more than symbolic; it should be a functioning organization designed to fulfill three purposes.

First, it should record past, present and anticipated studies of companies; giving information on sponsorship, time budget and instruments used. It should also track state and federal compliance reviews, as well as state fair employment investigations. One of the most vexing problems in this study--and similar studies--is the confusion and loss of respondent rapport engendered by the simultaneous conduct with the same companies of studies on equal employment by a number of researchers. Equal employment research is gaining greater support and interest. The companies that will cooperate form a select circle. The end result is that researchers frequently are on each other's heels in contacting the same organizations for interviews. The research problems investigated tend to overlap, and the same questions are frequently asked of the same respondents. Added to this is the possibility that a respondent may have answered the same questions and supplied the same data to a variety of agencies with quasilegal or legal jurisdiction. This multiplicity of efforts frequently undermines the effectiveness of the respondent interview. Some control of the research traffic is necessary.

Second, such a facility should store landmark data to provide the researcher with reference points for his research. All too frequently, earlier interviews conducted at a company by another researcher are inaccessible, making it difficult to view the research in historical depth. Recognizing the legal rights protecting government compliance data, it should still be feasible to make considerable data from public and private sources available.

Finally, there should be dissemination of information from research reports to a wide audience in clear and concise language familiar to the layman. This goal is not adequately filled by any resource at present.

(2) The study of equal employment practices in companies should not be undertaken without sufficient assurance that data on minority group profiles and employment structure will be available. Anecdotal data on equal employment practices have limited value; such data cannot be a substitute for information on structural characteristics (e.g., promotion rates, testing score distributions or training participation rates). Such data are hard to obtain in the aggregate for industry and certainly are very difficult to obtain for a single company by university or private researchers. The absence of such data makes equal employment assessment studies difficult, if not impossible. Some consideration must be given to this problem before undertaking such research.

(3) Related to the previous point, equal employment research in companies must be directed toward the evaluation of specific company practices and techniques that comprise affirmative action. A sufficient body of information had already been inventoried on problems and practices within a company context, but little attention has been paid to the funding of evaluation research to determine the relative effectiveness of a given practice or technique in equalizing opportunities. Any of the following questions would be good subjects for evaluation research. What is the effectiveness of different recruitment appeals in the Negro community? What is the efficacy of various test inventories in predicting the performance of Negroes in work situations? To what extent do various forms of training sponsored by the company reduce the handicaps of the Negro worker? How do different forms of management-to-worker communication affect the level of information on equal employment policy among the workers? What differences in effectiveness are there between the same techniques used in a number of different studies?

There is a particular need for research in selection techniques and evaluation of these techniques. The whole selection process for workers in industry--Negro and white--leaves many unanswered questions. Testing is only a small part of the total selection process, yet little research exists on the evaluation of interviews and personal background investigations as factors in selection decisions.

(4) There is a need to fund experimental and demonstration research into untried practices that may be influential in equalizing opportunities.  Of particular importance is the initiation of research into hiring, suspending traditional criteria of selection.  A number of workers might be placed in jobs who had unsatisfactory scores and their work performance compared with hirees who have successfully passed the tests.  Some attempt might also be made to see how innovative program-learning techniques might be used to increase the skill potential of undertrained workers.

(5) The perspective on equal employment research should shift from an emphasis on studies of company practices to a concern with Negro workers and their experiences with equal employment practices of companies.  It should be recognized that the attitudes and values of white and Negro workers may be active ingredients that modify the intent of the best company practices. We need to know more about them.  It is also in the work experiences of the Negro and white that we have the best evidence that practices intended to modify behavior are efficacious.  We must know more about the Negro worker in the labor market, how his job aspirations are shaped in the work situation and how he views his job problems.

(6) We need research on effectiveness criteria of equal employment programs.  How do we measure success or failure? How do these criteria differ by size of company, industry and location? What alternate criteria might be suggested as guidelines?

(7) Research is needed that goes beyond the concerns of the Negro in the company context.  Many of the Negro's reactions on the job are shaped by events, conditions and experiences that antedate their job situation.  Three kinds of studies would be useful to fill this knowledge gap.  First, some intensive profiles of the educational and social experiences of the Negro worker predating his entrance into the work world would be important.  Such studies should collect data on structural barriers to job preparations as well as the attitudes that emerge therefrom.  Second, we need studies of community structure and processes as determinants of prevocational preparation opportunities for workers.  Communities differ in the allocation of services to minority groups as well as in the availability of employment aids (e.g., private nonsegregated training facilities).  These patterns would give us new insights into the services (supplementary, compensatory or remedial) needed by Negro workers before opportunities can truly be equalized.

(8) We have reached a stage in equal employment research at which we must avail ourselves of new research perspectives as well as methods.  More comparative research should be initiated, possibly using federal compliance data to analyze discrimination patterns by employment structure, industry and community.  It would also be useful to compare the rate of development of equal

employment practices over time among comparable groups of companies.   Students of organizational analysis have developed numerous theories and tools to study both of these problems, and certainly such perspectives could considerably increase understanding of the application of equal employment practices.   The study of equal employment opportunities in a company setting is largely a study of organizations and how they operate.   The failure to utilize organizational theory to analyze these problems has left many questions unanswered in past research.

APPENDIXES

# APPENDIX A

## THE SELECTION PROCEDURES: COMPANIES AND INDIVIDUALS

APPENDIX A      THE SELECTION PROCEDURES:
                COMPANIES AND INDIVIDUALS


The twenty companies finally included in the research were not selected randomly from all companies in the nation. Before the study began, a number of decisions were made about the kinds of companies that could most profitably be used to study the dynamics and processes associated with equal employment opportunity programs. In general terms, the following selection criteria were used. The companies included should each have a public image or stance of trying to promote an equal employment opportunity program. The companies should represent a variety of employment structures. The companies should be representative of growing industrial sectors of the economy with evidence of job possibilities for Negroes. And the companies should represent a good regional spread. It had also been planned to study a single plant over time, but time rebudgeting problems eliminated this possibility.

Necessity forced us to compromise these criteria. In the final selection, we were dependent on the decisions of these companies to cooperate and participate in the study. We anticipated that there would be refusals and thus began with a list of eighty-three companies. Each of these companies was included because it filled one or more of the criteria and because there was a reasonable prospect of cooperation. Through outright refusals or reconsideration, the list was narrowed to forty-four companies (see Appendix Table 1). At the corporate headquarters of each company, Schedules I and IA were administered. The end result produced twenty-seven corporate interviews and complete information on each category of inquiry. The final twenty companies were selected from this list.

The twenty companies represent a variety of employment structures and vary in size, number of branch units, geographical spread and product or service. A central commitment in the study was to maintain the anonymity of the unit to encourage the most frank and open expression of attitudes and opinions by corporate and local plant officials. The following descriptions give pertinent facts about the concerns without the violation of information that might be used to identify the company:

161

APPENDIX TABLE 1

DISTRIBUTION OF REASONS GIVEN BY THIRTY-NINE
COMPANIES FOR NONPARTICIPATION IN STUDY

|  | Number |
|---|---|
| Integration is too recent; study might upset long-run plan; study might disturb recently integrated work force. | 15 |
| Too busy; study would interfere with duties of employees. | 11 |
| Company had already engaged in a recent study or compliance review. | 5 |
| No reason specified. | 5 |
| Key personnel preparing for collective bargaining. | 3 |

Company 1:  Transportation service, both domestic and international.  Terminals in every major city in the United States are staffed predominantly with female employees.  There are twelve major transportation service centers with predominantly male employees in the craft trades.  The service crews of the vehicles include both male and female employees.  Three separate unions hold jurisdiction over the service crews.

A terminal unit in a major southern city was selected for study. Employment was predominantly female.

Company 2:  Major utility in a border city of the South.  The maintenance crews are unionized and predominantly male.  In selected installations, female workers predominate.  About 25 per cent of the work crews are Negro, and about 21 per cent of the clerical and service female workers are Negroes.

Company 3:  Small concern specializing in the manufacture of electronic equipment as well as in research and development work.  In the last 10 years, total employment has fluctuated between 900 and 2,100 workers.  About 60 per cent of the employment is male, either in technical or professional work.  The company has only one location in a small midwestern community of 21,000 people.

Company 4:  Moderately large retail department store chain in the east northcentral states.  There are forty-seven branches located in three states.  Employment of the sales force is overwhelmingly female and about evenly divided between part-time and full-time employees.  The firm is family-owned.

Company 5:  Major manufacturer and servicer of radio, television and electronic equipment.  It has manufacturing and service installations in seventy cities.  In its manufacturing operations, there is a heavy concentration of semiskilled female workers, flanked by a light number of male unskilled and craft workers. Service centers are franchised.

Company 6:  Major food processor and distributor.  Plants are located in thirty-five communities in the United States.  There are also a number of installations in foreign countries.  The sex ratio varies from installation to installation, but women predominate in processing operations and men in the distribution and sales divisions.

Company 7:  Major food distributor in retail outlets in the United States.  It operates retail outlets, some franchised, in almost every U.S. community with a population over 20,000.  Local employment practices vary, with unionization in some stores but not in others.  Part-time help is largely female, while full-time workers are predominantly male.  Turnover is less than 7 per cent in any given year.

Company 8:  Major processor of rolled steel, operating large plants in the midwestern area.  The size of the plants varies from 1,400 employees to over 15,000 workers.  The work force is predominantly male and represents the complete range of skills in metal processing operations.

Company 9:  Major manufacturer of electronic equipment, with plants located in twenty-six communities across the United States. The workers possess a high level of technical training, and semi-skilled operatives are rigorously selected for employment.

Company 10:  Leading manufacturer of heavy machinery in the United States.  Plants are in the Midwest and the South.  Plant work forces range from 1,800 to over 12,000 workers.  The work force is composed largely of semiskilled male operatives.

Company 11:  Leader in aerospace research and manufacturing.  Plants are located in the South and in the West.  The work force is largely composed of male technicians and semiskilled operatives.

Company 12:  Leading utility in a large midwestern community. The equipment crews are male; the clerical and service workers are largely female.

Company 13:  Single-plant producer and servicer of office equipment in the northeastern United States.  About two-thirds of the work force are women engaged in semiskilled operative work.  The work force totals 2,100 employees.

Company 14: National and international manufacturer and distributor of a variety of electronic equipment. There are twelve major plants located in the Northeast and Midwest. The work force in manufacturing is largely female semiskilled operatives, flanked by male craft and unskilled workers.

Company 15: Major processor of food. It operates a single processing complex located in the southern states. The work force is 60 per cent male, and the work is predominantly semiskilled. The company employs 3,600 workers.

Company 16: Producer of food and beverage products. The company is family-owned and operates a single manufacturing complex in a northern city. The work force is predominantly male and is organized in craft unions.

Company 17: Major producer of electrical equipment, with 7 plants across the United States. The smallest plant employs 800 workers; the largest employs over 9,500 workers. Females predominate by a slight margin in the semiskilled jobs, the largest employment category.

Company 18: Manufacturer of transportation equipment in a small southern city. The work force totals 1,800 and is nonunion, except for selected crafts. The work force is overwhelming male.

Company 19: Small tool and die shop in a large northern city. The shop employs eighty-six workers and is nonunion. More than four fifths of the work force are in skilled craft jobs.

Company 20: Large distributor of petroleum products in the midwestern states. The retail outlets employ males exclusively, with about 65 per cent of the work force on a part-time basis.

Although these twenty companies represent a variety of employment situations, they are not a random selection of all employment situations. As originally conceived, we felt that the list should include a chemical manufacturing company. Although two were available, they offered resistance to participation in the study and were bypassed. On the nonmanufacturing side, we sought banking and insurance institutions. We examined several possibilities and gained valuable insights into the equal employment problems of such units. For a number of reasons, these units were bypassed in favor of others. We sought entrance to a number of service establishments--restaurants and hotels--but particular circumstances intruded, and we had to eliminate these possibilities. The twenty companies do represent, we believe, a range of employment experiences and structures that publicly profess an equal employment opportunity philosophy.

## THE SELECTION OF INDIVIDUAL PARTICIPANTS
## AND GROUPS FROM THE COMPANIES

Each company participated in the study by providing us with certain required data from its administrative records and memos and by having a number of members from different groups and positions participate in the study as individual respondents, i.e., answer the questionnaires and interviews we have developed. The selection of individual respondent was made by the study's research staff and was dictated by the objectives of the research project.

Even before selecting the appropriate individuals, a decision had to be made as to which of the many groups and subgroups of personnel should participate in the study. The companies were too large to have all workers represented, and the resources of the project made it difficult to draw a random sample of the whole company in sufficient size to guarantee representativeness. This last consideration also made it difficult to make comparisons of representative samples between companies. It was thought that this problem could be made manageable by sharply defining the categories of workers to be questioned and by treating the white and Negro workers selected as representative samples of these kinds of workers in these twenty companies. The limitations of the study should be kept in mind. First, not all workers in these companies were in the pool from which the selection was made. Second, there are not twenty discrete samples, each one of which is large enough to make comparisons across companies. Third, the sample selection from the worker categories is random and scientific. Thus, we can talk about Negro workers and white workers in these categories and be reasonably certain, with limitations noted, that their views are representative of all Negroes and whites in these categories in the twenty companies. Since the selection of the companies was not random the workers discussed in this report cannot be said to be representative of all workers in integrated firms.

### Occupational Categories for Selection

In the study, we desired to portray the attitudes of a number of groups in many different kinds of employment structures. The single central idea of the study was to obtain depth data that could be used to give some idea of the processes and underlying dynamics confronted in a work integration study. For this purpose, intensive depth interviewing was undertaken, using the specially designed instruments that have been described.

Five broad occupational categories were selected: professional and technical workers; white-collar (clerical and sales)

workers;   craft   workers;   semiskilled   workers;   unskilled workers.

(1) <u>Professional and technical workers</u>.   College or advanced
technical training was required for these jobs.   In some cases,
these workers held administrative titles.   Operationally, the group
was defined by a listing of such personnel supplied by the company.

(2) <u>White-collar (clerical and sales) workers.</u>  We restricted
ourselves to full-time workers with three years of service for
whites and at least eighteen months for Negroes.   Using the <u>Dic-
tionary of Occupational Titles</u> as a guide, we restricted ourselves
to work that needed no special preparation and could be learned on
the job.   This encompassed the range of lower-level clerical skills
for which typing was the major requirement.

(3) <u>Craft workers</u>. These included any jobs that were apprenticeable   and   required craft training.   Eliminated were jobs
where craft functions were performed without credentials.

(4) <u>Semiskilled workers</u>. These jobs needed no specialized
training. We restricted ourselves to white employees with at least
three years of service and Negroes with at least eighteen months
of service.

(5) <u>Unskilled workers</u>.   These were the lowest jobs in the
company, requiring no preparation.   We limited ourselves to
whites with three years of service and Negroes with at least
eighteen months of service.

In a number of companies, some of these jobs did not exist.
After an enumeration had been obtained for   each category in the
company, an appropriate sampling ratio was assigned.   In some
cases, the number of workers in the category was so small as to
make it necessary to include all workers in the category. The
sampling ratios were computed, and each respondent was randomly
drawn from the category.   The procedure was first utilized for the
white workers and then the Negro workers. This resulted in a sample
of 501 white workers and 335 Negro workers.

THE INTERVIEWING OF NEGRO RESPONDENTS

Early in the formulation of the research plan, it was decided
to assign Negro interviewers to Negro respondents.  Our logic was
that Negro respondents would be much more frank in their responses
to questions from Negroes than to questions from whites.  In order
to  test this  proposition, we  selected twenty Negro respondents
who were not to be in our study sample and interviewed them twice,
using shortened pretest versions of Schedule IV. The first interview

was conducted by a white interviewer and the second by a Negro interviewer. The project director and three graduate assistants examined both sets of questionnaires, noting similarities and differences in response patterns. We attempted to isolate four distinct themes in the interview for comparison: views regarding racial employment patterns in the company; tendencies to blame whites in general for inequalities in jobs and opportunities; views regarding how much was being done to help the Negro to equal job opportunity; and future prospects for equalizing employment opportunities. A comparison of both sets of interviews is made in Appendix Table 2.

These results indicate that the information supplied by Negroes to white interviewers can be markedly different from that supplied to Negro interviewers. Using white interviewers, the response patterns indicate a tendency to deny the existence of racial employment patterns or that whites are responsible for job inequalities. There is also a tendency for Negro response patterns to be optimistic in discussing the prospects for equalizing job opportunities with white interviewers. With Negro interviewers, Negro respondents were quick to criticize racial employment practices, to blame whites for the inequalities, to deny that anything significant was being done to help them. They revealed also definite pessimism regarding future prospects for equal employment opportunities.

The examination of these two sets of responses suggest the following. Negro respondents structured their responses to the white interviewers to deny the existence of job inequalities or that employment offered them any special problems. Response patterns accentuated positive aspects of the work situation and avoided real discussion of problem areas. "There is nothing wrong" and "I am getting along fine" were their fairly normative and frequent responses to white interviewers. On the other hand, Negro respondents gave considerable emphasis to the race problems in employment and stressed the need for change and amelioration of certain discrimination practices when Negro interviewers were used. These observations suggest that different response patterns, both exaggerated but in different directions, may be forthcoming depending on the race of the interviewer. It is possible that the Negro feels that his personal job distresses must be kept from the white interviewer; thus, interviews become problem-free in content. In talking to Negro interviewers, there may be a need to deny that anything is going right, since the prevailing Negro climate of opinion emphasizes the high level of inequality between Negro and white job opportunities. The response patterns in such interviews may give inordinate emphasis to the problems for Negroes in the work situation without noting the aspects in which improvement has occurred.

## COMPARISON OF RESPONSE PATTERNS OF TWENTY NEGROES
### USING NEGRO AND WHITE INTERVIEWERS

| | Response to Negro Interviewers | Response to White Interviewers |
|---|---|---|
| Theme 1: Views regarding racial employment patterns in the company: | | |
| "Improvement needed." | 18 | 4 |
| "Negro is disadvantaged." | 20 | 6 |
| "More opportunity at this company than at others." | 9 | 14 |
| "Whites have better opportunities to get ahead." | 19 | 4 |
| Theme 2: Tendencies to blame whites for inequalities in jobs and opportunities. | | |
| "Whites take advantage of the Negro in this company." | 19 | 4 |
| "Whites are responsible for poor job opportunities." | 20 | 2 |
| Theme 3: How much was being done to help the Negro equalize opportunities. | | |
| "Nothing is being done." | 12 | 6 |
| Theme 4: Future prospects for equalizing opportunities. | | |
| "Optimistic." | 4 | 11 |
| "Pessimistic." | 16 | 9 |

The use of Negro interviewers invites the danger of obtaining a portrait of equal employment opportunities that is weighted toward the negative side. The Negro interviews in this study cannot be considered without reference to the response patterns obtained from the white workers, corporate officials, union leaders and local plant officers. Negro responses--indeed, any of the responses--gain significance only in relation to the total set of data in this study.

## NONRESPONSE PATTERNS AMONG NEGRO
## AND WHITE RESPONDENTS

It has already been indicated that high nonresponse rates occurred among both Negro and white respondents. It would be well to examine nonresponse patterns and discuss their implications for the present study. Three possible explanations for nonresponse will be discussed: the national climate of the civil rights movement; problems of field administration; and the social characteristics of the respondents. Let us discuss each one in turn:

(1) <u>The national climate of the civil rights movement.</u> The field interviewing was conducted at a time when there was a strong civil rights tide. Legislation for equal voting was in process. The Civil Rights Act was imminent. Selma and Montgomery were in the news. It may have been this national climate that predisposed many whites to remain silent in this study. For the most part, white respondents were reticent in the interviews, suggesting that the current climate may have predisposed the integration-prone whites to respond with caution and, at the same time, to dissuade the anti-integration whites from responding.

(2) <u>Problems of field administration.</u> At the beginning of the study, the plan had been to use professional interviewers from the Survey Research Center Interviewer Network. We felt rather strongly that many of the delicate and sensitive question areas required interviewers of long experience and adequate preparation. Our decision to use Negro interviewers to interview Negroes and white interviewers to interview whites has already been explained. However, the distribution of plant locations permitted us to use professional interviewers only in some of the cases. In some locations where the Survey Interviewer Network did not reach, we were forced to recruit nonprofessional interviewers. A training program for interviewers was established, but it did not result in the availability of professional interviewers. For a variety of reasons, the attrition rate of these interviewers was high, especially among Negro students, who deserted in great numbers to participate in civil rights activity in Selma. Additional training sessions were held, but the quality of candidates was low in these new groups; the high nonresponse rate may be a reflection of these problems.

In at least two plants, another factor contributed to the non-response rate. The plant officials refused to permit home interviews and insisted on interviews on plant premises. There were several indications from respondent comments that such situations were not comfortable and were actually anxiety-producing. Although the total list of names was frequently given to the researchers, there was definite pressure in many company situations not to "push" respondents for interviews. Undoubtedly, many of our nonprofessional interviewers fared badly in these situations.

(3) The social characteristics of the respondents. The data in Appendix Table 3 indicate that nonresponse varied with the social characteristics of the respondents. Among the whites, the typical nonrespondent was female, older than forty years of age and engaged in unskilled work; had failed to complete high school; and resided in one of the southern or border states. Among Negroes, the characteristics of nonrespondents differed in several respects. The typical Negro nonrespondent was male, over forty years of age and in a job category requiring some skill; had completed high school; and resided in one of the southern or border states. In both groups, the differences between respondents and nonrespondents is striking. What do these differences suggest about the nonresponse patterns in this study?

First, older respondents--whether white or Negro--were more reluctant to participate in the study than younger respondents. In two recent studies of the Survey Research Center at The University of Michigan, samples of Negro workers showed the same nonresponse patterns, although not to the degree in this study. Younger Negroes showed a higher response rate. Two factors may be involved here. First, younger Negroes tend to be better educated and less reticent in general about verbalizing personal feelings about race. Second, older respondents obviously have more of an investment in traditional employment practices and are less willing to discuss aspects of Negro exclusion.

Among whites, it was the less educated who did not respond, whereas, among the Negroes, it was the more educated who did not respond. It was an observation made time and time again in this study that the Negroes in lower-skilled jobs were more cooperative in the study and more open in responses than Negroes in better jobs. It was apparent that, for many Negroes, the interview situation provided an opportunity to tell a sympathetic outsider their grievances--real or imagined. Negroes in higher-status jobs were not openly critical because, in a sense, they had achieved in this system.

Finally, whites and Negroes in the South were less willing to participate than their counterparts in the North. As we indicated, the interviewing period was one of confusion and mass demonstration in the South, a factor undoubtedly promoting nonresponse.

## APPENDIX TABLE 3

### CHARACTERISTICS OF RESPONDENTS
### AND NONRESPONDENTS BY RACE[a]

| | Whites | | Negroes | |
|---|---|---|---|---|
| | Respondent | Non-respondent | Respondent | Non-respondent |
| Males | 85% | 64% | 63% | 84% |
| Under 40 years of Age | 75 | 63 | 60 | 39 |
| Low-skilled[b] | 18 | 35 | 87 | 64 |
| Less than Completion of high school | 35 | 64 | 65 | 53 |
| Residing in border or southern state | 29 | 44 | 31 | 20 |

a Of the 501 white workers who had been selected, 205 answered the questionnaire (41%); 215 (64%) of the 335 Negroes responded.

b Includes only blue-collar low-skilled. See Table 3 for definition.

Beyond this, however, many of our interviewers observed that respondents who resided in the South did not perceive pressures for equal employment in their work situations and would frequently dismiss the subject as being without substance. It should be recalled that, at this time, Section VII of the Civil Rights Act was not yet a reality, and few southerners--white or Negro--were really subjected to pressures for change.

## METHODOLOGICAL LIMITATIONS

Perhaps the most serious limitation was the restriction of the sample of companies. There was no control over who would participate, and it must be stated quite emphatically that the twenty companies selected are not fully representative. However, the companies are sufficiently diverse in structure, location and employment structure as to present a variety of equal employment opportunity situations.

A second limitation stems from the fact that resources did not permit a large enough sample to make a number of subgroup comparisons. Nor was it possible to compare across companies and to relate program to structure. These are certainly goals for further research. The present study aims at isolating insights and concepts to lay the foundation for further research.

Finally, the low response rate is a barrier to generalizing these results. The interview and respondent factors that led to this low response rate must be kept in mind in interpretation of the data in the present study.

APPENDIX B

PROFILE OF STUDY COMPANIES

## APPENDIX TABLE 4

## PROFILE OF STUDY COMPANIES

| Company | Location of Corporate Headquarters | Location of Branch Unit Studied | No. of Employees in Branch Unit | No. of Negroes in Branch Unit Studied | | Product or Service |
|---|---|---|---|---|---|---|
| | | | | White-Collar* | Blue-Collar** | |
| 1. | New York City | Nashville, Tenn. | 56 | 3 | - | Transportation service |
| 2. | Washington, D.C. | Washington, D.C. | 137 | 38 | 5 | Utility |
| 3. | Small community in central Illinois | Small community in central Illinois | 1,040 | 10 | 58 | Electronics |
| 4. | Detroit, Mich. | Large city in the Midwest | 97 | 19 | 10 | Utility |
| 5. | New York City | Small community in Midwest | 653 | 1 | 14 | Electronics and electrical manufacturing |
| 6. | Large eastern city | Large city in the South | 706 | 2 | 250 | Food processing |
| 7. | Large eastern city | Large city in the Midwest | 39 | - | 3 | Food distributor |
| 8. | Chicago, Illinois | Medium-size city in Indiana | 4,155 | 116 | 3,281 | Steel processing |
| 9. | Large eastern city | Medium-size city in the South | 3,507 | 33 | 55 | Electrical manufacturing |
| 10. | Chicago, Illinois | Medium-size city in the South | 4,059 | 4 | 659 | Transportation manufacturing |
| 11. | Western city | Western city | 5,003 | 135 | 1,231 | Transportation manufacturing |

APPENDIX TABLE 4 (con.)

| Company | Location of Corporate Headquarters | Location of Branch Unit Studied | No. of Employees in Branch Unit | No. of Negroes in Branch Unit Studied | | Product or Service |
|---|---|---|---|---|---|---|
| | | | | White-Collar* | Blue-Collar** | |
| 12. | Midwest city | Midwest city | 800 | 35 | 58 | Utility manufacturing |
| 13. | New England city | New England city | 2,579 | 62 | 71 | Manufacturing of office equipment |
| 14. | Northern city | Northern city | 2,702 | 12 | 83 | Electronics manufacturing |
| 15. | Southern city | Southern city | 2,300 | 3 | 208 | Food processing |
| 16. | Northern city | Northern city | 3,432 | 36 | 28 | Beverage |
| 17. | Northern city | Midwestern city | 5,992 | 10 | 700 | Electronics |
| 18. | Small southern city | Small southern city | 1,850 | 2 | 89 | Transportation manufacturing |
| 19. | Detroit, Michigan | Detroit, Michigan | 86 | – | 2 | Tool and die shop |
| 20. | Midwestern city | Midwestern city | 127 | 2 | 10 | Petroleum distributors |

\* Professional, technical, clerical, supervisory and skilled workers.
\*\* Unskilled, semiskilled and service workers.

# APPENDIX C

## RESEARCH SCHEDULES

RESEARCH
SCHEDULES

SCHEDULE I

CORPORATE QUESTIONNAIRE

Employment Structure and Policy of the Company

Would you say that your company has developed a fairly definite employment policy?

IF YES, ASK:
Is this policy written? (If yes: OBTAIN COPY.)
What are the major provisions of this policy?
Approximately how long has this policy been in effect?
____years.
Is this policy periodically reviewed? (If yes: How many times has it been reviewed in the last five years?)

Does your employment policy contain any provisions for equal employment opportunities for Negroes?

IF YES, ASK:
When were these provisions added to your employment policy?
What is the substance of these provisions?
Were there any special circumstances that led to the insertion of these provisions? (If yes: Can you describe these special circumstances?) (Get full details.)
(CHECK AND SEE IF COPIES OF COMPANY DIRECTIVES ON EQUAL EMPLOYMENT OPPORTUNITY PROGRAMS ARE AVAILABLE.)

From your viewpoint, what have been the major problems in administering this program in your company? (Can you give me the details?)

Are you aware of any special problems that are faced by your local managers in the (divisions, plants) of your company in administering the policy? (If yes, can you give me the details?)

How about your first-line supervisors (e.g., foremen or office managers)? Are you aware of any special problems that they have faced in administering the Equal Employment Opportunity program? (If yes, can you give me the details?)

History of the Equal Employment Opportunities Program

When was the first time that the company hired Negroes in other than low-level or unskilled work?

When did the company adopt its present policy on Negro employment?

What were the circumstances that led to the adoption of the present policy?

Was the decision to develop an Equal Employment Opportunity program associated with a particular person or group in the company?

IF YES:
Who?
Can you give me a brief sketch of (his, their) beliefs that led (him, them) to take this initiative?
Can you be specific about (his, their) other views that may have influenced this decision?
Are these views widely shared in top levels of the company, or are there people who have different views? If different views, can you tell me about them?

Looking back on the program in your company, do any special problems come to mind that developed in the implementation of the program?

IF YES:
Can you tell me about them?
How were they handled?
What alternatives were considered?

Are there any other problems that occurred in the development or implementation of the program?

IF YES, ASK:
Can you tell me about them?

Have any of the procedures that you developed in initially implementing your equal employment program been modified since that time?

IF YES, ASK:
In what way?

For each change, can you indicate the approximate date of change and the major considerations that led to the change?

Let me be more specific. What changes have taken place in the following since the initial development of the Equal Employment Opportunity program in your company?
Recruiting
Training

      Upgrading
      Grievance handling
      Compliance control

## Corporate Administration of the Equal Employment Opportunity Program

Who are the people in the corporate headquarters primarily responsible for the administration of the program? (Titles)

Does top administrator of the program report to a higher authority? (If yes: What is the title and department of higher authority?)

Does more than one department share responsibility for the program? (If yes: What departments?)

Typically, in the local units of your company, what individual by title is responsible for:
      hiring
      promotions
      selection for management training
      selection for higher skill training
      handling of grievances

In the administration of a personnel program in your company, what is the usual procedure of policy enforcement?

Are there any informal procedures used by corporate headquarters to check compliance in the divisions? (e.g., telephone conversations, informal chats?)
If yes, give details.
How frequently are these informal checks made?

Does any group at corporate headquarters review the implementation of the program?

## Employee Recruitment

Can you briefly describe the recruitment practices that are typical of your local (plants, divisions)?

Does the company have relative freedom in hiring, or is it bound to certain patterns (e.g., priority to a recall list)? (GET DETAILS.)

Has this interfered in any way with the active development of your program? If yes, in what ways?

Very frequently a company has to "reach out" into the Negro community to recruit applicants. Has this been your company's experience?

IF YES:
What specific activities has your company developed to recruit Negro workers?    (e.g., recruiting at Negro colleges,
contacting local Negro leaders, etc.)

Has your company experienced any difficulty in hiring trained
Negroes?

IF YES:
Can you tell me about these difficulties?
Why do you think there is an insufficient number of trained
Negroes?  (PROBE.)

## Grievance and Discipline Control

Some questions about the handling of grievances and discipline
in your company.

At what level of your company are most employee grievances
and complaints handled?  (Get details.)

Are Negro complaints and grievances handled at the same
level?  (If not, at what supervisory level are they handled?)

Are there any special measures taken by corporate headquarters when grievances are filed by Negroes?    (If yes, what
measures?)

Is there a special appeal or grievance procedure available to
Negro employees?  (If yes, can you tell me about it?)

Are there any groups, formal or informal, which serve to
represent Negro employees in a (plant, division) of your company?

IF YES:
PROBE:    What kind of group is that?  (e.g., Negro worker
committee, Negro union local biracial committee to deal
with human relations problems)

## Community Relationships

Based on your company's experience, what characteristics of
a local work force impede or facilitate the development of an Equal
Employment Opportunity program?  (e.g., skill makeup, region, etc.
GET SPECIFIC DETAILS.)

Some of our respondents report that care must be taken to
tailor a program to a given community.  Has your company found
it necessary to vary the program to fit different communities?

Some companies have an active policy of encouraging their executives to involve themselves in community affairs, while other companies frown on such involvement. What is the current practice on this in your company? How is it related to your Equal Employment Opportunity policy?

Does the executive file any kind of activity reports on his contacts or community work?
What is in these reports?
Who reviews this report?

## Unions

Do you have a union in any of your installations?

IF YES:
Which union is that? (Are there any others?)
What effect do you feel that your Equal Employment Opportunity program has had on this union? (Get details)
(If international union) Was the international involved in the development of your program? (If yes, in what ways?)
Were locals involved in the initiation of the policy? If yes, give details.

## Background information

Name of interviewee
His position with the company
How long has he been with the company?
How long has he been associated with the Equal Employment Opportunity program?
Age
Present business address.

## SCHEDULE II

## EMPLOYMENT PRACTICES IN LOCAL PLANTS

Total number of employees in (        ) (assigned unit) for the pay period nearest the date of this interview: _____

Total number of Negro employees (same unit, same date): _____

In which of these general categories do Negroes work at present? (Checklist)
Unskilled blue-collar (including service jobs)_____
Skilled blue-collar (craft or semitechnical jobs)_____
White-collar (clerical or office jobs)_____
Professional or technical _____
Other (specify) _____

IF NEGROES ARE EMPLOYED IN JOBS ABOVE "UNSKILLED," ASK:

> What specific jobs are held by these Negroes?
> Are these male or female workers?
> When were they first hired on these jobs?

IF NEGROES ARE NOT EMPLOYED IN JOBS ABOVE "UN-SKILLED," ASK:

Why is it that Negro workers have not been placed in these jobs? (Probe: qualifications, aptitude and availability of Negro workers for these jobs; his assessment of Negro worker potential for these jobs.)

In bringing a worker into your company, who does the actual hiring; in other words, who makes the final decision? (Probe: not the name of the person but his title.)
> Are any checks made on this person's decisions? (If yes, can you tell me about them?)
> Do incoming workers take any kind of tests? (If yes, which tests; what are their purposes?)
> Do you have minimum standards for hiring a worker? (If yes, can you tell me about them?)

Let me ask you some questions about your upgrading procedures and policies. First, what kind of seniority do you have? (Probe: craft, job, department, plants or other?)
> Is seniority lost when shifting from one job to another?
> What about the lines of progression in this plant--is it necessary to shift from one line of progression to another to get to a more skilled job?
> Is seniority lost when shifting from one line of progression to another?
> What part is played by on-the-job training in moving from lower-to higher-skilled jobs in your company? Can you tell me about that?
> How about bidding for jobs; is this a practice in your company? (If yes, can you tell me about it?)
> Are there any formalized controls that guide selections in on-the-job training and/or bidding? (If yes, can you tell me about them?)

Has the development of a nondiscriminatory policy introduced any new procedures into your employment practices? (If yes, can you tell me about them?)
> (Probe: Are there any monitoring or policing procedures in hiring, training or promoting?)

What special procedures of compliance and reporting have been adopted with respect to the Equal Employment Opportunity policy?
> Are written progress reports submitted by the divisions?
> What information is contained in these reports?
> How frequently are these reports submitted?

Are there any informal procedures used by your staff to check compliance in the divisions? (e.g., telephone conversations, informal chats?)
IF YES, give details.
How frequently are these informal checks made?

How did you come to decide on the particular approach that you are following in the enforcement of this policy?
What alternatives did you consider?
What considerations governed your decision?

Looking back on your own experiences with a nondiscrimination policy, what advice would you give to a company that was just beginning to hire Negroes? (Probe: employment and policing procedures)

Suppose that you were asked to suggest some ways in which Negro employment opportunities could be improved. What specific suggestions might you make? (Probe: Role of Federal and state government and local community authorities)

## SCHEDULE IIA

## LOCAL PLANT QUESTIONNAIRE

What problems did you anticipate prior to the adoption of these minority group employment practices? Please rank order each item according to the following scale:
+++ would be a major problem
++ would be some problem
+ would be a minor problem
0 would be no problem at all
___ a. resistance by white workers
___ b. lack of qualified Negroes to fill available jobs
___ c. interference with productivity or worker efficiency
___ d. community opposition
___ e. poor customer relations where Negroes had to deal with whites
___ f. resistance by supervisors
___ g. Negro dissatisfaction with available job opportunities
___ h. resistance by the union
___ i. Other (please specify) _____

Looking back since the development of these practices, which of these problems, if any, did occur? Please rank order each item according to the following scale:
+++ became a major problem
++ became somewhat of a problem
+ became a minor problem
0 was no problem at all
___ a. resistance by white workers
___ b. lack of qualified Negroes to fill available jobs

___ c.   interference with productivity or worker efficiency
___ d.   community opposition
___ e.   poor customer relations where Negroes had to deal with whites
___ f.   resistance by supervisors
___ g.   Negro dissatisfaction with available job opportunities
___ h.   resistance by the union
___ i.   Other (please specify)_____

Which one of the following would be considered the best measure of success by your company in a program of equal employment opportunity?   Please rank order according to the following scale:
+++ best single measure
++ a good measure
+ a minor consideration in success
0 not a consideration at all
___ a.   number of Negro employees in relation to number of Negroes in the local community
___ b.   distribution of Negroes through job classifications
___ c.   the income level of the Negroes in the company
___ d.   the visibility of Negroes in company jobs
___ e.   job mobility of Negroes in the company
___ f.   the presence of Negro employees in the management, technical or supervisory levels of the company
___ g.   the number of entry jobs that have been filled by Negroes
___ h.   Other (please specify)_____

What special practices or programs, if any, have been developed by your company as part of the equal employment opportunity program? (Please describe briefly, if applicable).
a.   Recruitment practices or programs
b.   Training practices or programs
c.   Testing practices or programs
d.   Placement practices or programs
e.   Community programs
f.   If other practices or programs, please specify.

SCHEDULE III

WHITE WORKER AND SUPERVISOR QUESTIONNAIRE

## Job Mobility and Structure

First, let me ask you some questions about your job in this company.
How long have you worked for this company?
What did you do before you started to work here? (Job title, name of company, location, principal operation, size)

Have you had any promotions or has your responsibility increased since you started to work here?

IF YES:
What promotions did you have? (Changes in job title, responsibility and pay)
How long have you been in your present job?
How would you describe your present job to someone who knew nothing about it?
Job title
Responsibilities (e.g., record-keeping, supervision, etc.)
Required contact with other people at work.
Activity confined to one department or across department.
Actual activities on the job (What are the things that you do on the job? Do you perform a single operation or many?)

Consider your present job for the moment. Do you feel that your activities in the job are about the same as those of a Negro worker in the same job in the company?

IF NO:
In what ways are they different?

Training

Are there any special training programs sponsored by the company at the present time?

IF YES:
What kind of program(s) is this? (on-the-job, formal training, tuition-sponsored or other)
Do you think that personal characteristics play a role in admission to such programs? (If yes, what personal characteristics improve your chances, and which ones limit your chances?)

Equal Employment Policy

Does this company have an equal employment opportunity policy for Negroes?

IF YES, ASK:
Can you tell me something about this nondiscrimination policy? (Probe: anything else?)
How do you feel about the company's nondiscrimination policy? (Probe: Why do you feel this way?)
Do you think it was a mistake for the company to adopt a nondiscrimination policy? (If yes, can you tell me why?)

Has this company done anything special to hire Negroes for jobs?

IF YES:
  What have they done?
  Why have they done this?
  How do you feel about this?

Has this company done anything special to open up training opportunities for Negroes?

IF YES:
  What have they done?
  Why have they done this?
  How do you feel about it?

Has this company done anything special to guarantee Negroes better opportunities for promotion?

IF YES:
  What have they done?
  Why have they done this?
  How do you feel about it?

Interpersonal Relations at Work

In your present work situation, how many of the workers in your department are Negro?
About how many are white?

Suppose that you had to describe the people that you work with. Are they friendly and cooperative, or are they unfriendly and uncooperative?
In what ways?  (Record specific incidents)

We would like to know something about your recent contacts with Negroes in this company. As part of your job, do you regularly come into contact with Negroes?

IF YES:
  Do you consider any of these Negro workers to be:
    A close friend that you can talk over confidential matters
    with
            Yes _____    No _____
    A good friend to whom you can say what you really think
            Yes _____    No _____
    Someone who calls you by your first name
            Yes _____    No _____
    Someone you just know to speak to
            Yes _____    No _____

Has there been some particular experience at work during the last year that made you feel more favorable toward Negroes?

IF YES:
    PROBE:  Can you tell me about it?

Do Negroes in this company organize their own social activities, or do they carry them on jointly with whites?

## Images of the Negro Worker

Suppose that someone asked you to give them some idea of what Negro workers in this company are like. What would you tell him? (Probe: What are their good points and bad points?)

Do most of the other workers in this department share these impressions?    (If no, in what way are these other impressions different?)

Compared to white workers in the same job, how do Negro workers stack up?  Are they better, worse or about the same?

IF BETTER:
    In what ways are they better?

IF WORSE:
    In what ways are they worse?

Very often a Negro will seem to stay in the same job for years while a white worker hired in the same job at the same time will move ahead.  Why do you feel that this happens?
    What about yourself.   How do you personally feel about working with Negroes? (Can you tell me more about this?)

How do you think the people here would feel about working with a Negro supervisor? (Probe: What problems do you think a Negro supervisor might have in this company?)

Are there some jobs in this company that are mostly filled by Negro workers?

IF YES:
    Which ones? (Probe)
    Are there some jobs to which Negroes are directed when they are hired?  (If yes, can you tell me about them?)

Suppose that a Negro worker was to apply for a job in this company that had always been filled by a white worker. How do you think most of the white workers here would feel? (Probe: Why would they feel this way?)

Suppose that a Negro worker in this company asked a white worker to show him how a particular machine worked or how a job was done.  How do you think the white worker would react? (Probe)

Why do you think he would react in this way?
Would the white worker have reacted differently if another white worker had been involved?

## SCHEDULE IV

## NEGRO WORKER QUESTIONNAIRE

### Job Mobility and Structure

First, let me ask you some questions about your job in this company.

How long have you worked for this company?
What did you do before you started to work here? (Job title, name of company, location, principal operation, size)

Have you had any promotions or has your responsibility increased since you started to work here?

IF YES:
What promotions did you have? (Note changes in job titles, responsibilities and pay.)
Were these changes across departments or were they all within a single department? (Note departmental name.)

Has there been any important change in the kind of work you do since you started to work here?

IF YES:
What changes in the kind of work you do have occurred?
When did these changes take place?

How long have you been in your present job?

How would you describe your present job to someone who knows nothing about it? (Get a list of the activities that he does.)
_____ Job title
_____ Responsibilities (e.g., record-keeping, supervision, etc.)
_____ Required contact with other people at work
_____ Activity confined to one department or across several departments
_____ Actual activities on the job (What are the things that you do on the job? Do you perform a single operation or many operations.)

What is the title of your immediate supervisor on your present job?
Is this person white or Negro?

Is there anyone else that you report to--anyone else to whom you are directly responsible for your activities?
    IF YES, what is the title of that person?
    Is this person white or Negro?

## Training and Preparation for New Jobs

What is the highest grade of schooling that you completed?

Before you began working on a full-time basis, did you receive any special training or preparation for work?

Once you started to work on a full-time basis, did you receive any special training?
    IF YES, what was this training? (Get details)
    Was this on-the-job or off-the-job training?

How about your present job in this company; did you receive any special training for it?
    IF YES, can you describe this training?
    To what extent is this training being used in your present job?
    Have you received any other training in this company?
    (If yes, what training?)

How about yourself? Are you personally interested in taking any of the training courses sponsored by the company?
    IF YES, ASK: Which ones?
    Are you eligible for these training programs? (If no, what requirements do you lack?)
    Have you applied for the program? (If yes, with what results?)
    Have you been either encouraged or discouraged by anyone in the company? (If yes, who encouraged and/or who discouraged you?)

Have you discussed your interest in training with anyone in the company or anyone outside of the company? (Who were these people? What was their reaction--did they encourage or discourage you?)

## Recruitment and Initial Placement

How did you find out about the job opening in this company when you were first employed here? (Details)

How about your jobs before you came to work for this company-- how did you find out about those job openings?

What did you know about this company before you applied for a job here? (PROBE: wages, working conditions, promotional opportunities, training opportunities)

What did you know about this company's employment policies regarding Negroes? (Obtain details)
How did you find out about this?

Some people tell us that they have one or two key people that they consult about employment possibilities when looking for a job. Do you go to some particular person for this kind of help?
IF YES, who is this person or persons? (i.e., his relationship to you--be specific.)

Do you go to this person for any other kind(s) of information?

Suppose that you had to find a new job next week. How would you go about it? (Probe: use of employment service, leads from friends and relatives, other)
In your opinion, what is the most likely source of job leads for you?
What is the least likely source of job leads for you?

When you were first employed by this company, did you take any employment tests?

When you were first hired by this company, in what job were you placed?
In what department was this job?
How many Negroes besides yourself worked in that department?
Did your job involve contacts mostly with Negro workers or white workers or both about the same?
Did you feel that being a Negro placed limitations on the job that would not be so in the case of a white worker? (If yes, what were these limitations?)

When you were first hired by this company, did you feel that you were either underqualified or overqualified for the job in which you were placed?

Equal Employment Policy

Does this company have an equal employment opportunity policy for Negroes?
IF YES, ask, "Can you give me some of the details of this policy?" (Probe: anything else?)

Has this company done anything special to hire Negroes for jobs?
IF YES, what have they done?

Has this company done anything special to open up training opportunities for Negroes?
IF YES, what have they done?

Has this company done anything special to guarantee Negroes better opportunities for promotion?
If yes, what have they done?

Have all groups of Negro workers benefited equally from these company policies?
If not, which groups have benefited more than others? (e.g., white-collar workers)  Why do you feel that this is true?

How did you learn about the equal employment opportunity policy?

What has been your most important source of information about this policy?

## Interpersonal Relations at Work

We would like to know something about your recent contacts with whites in this company.  As part of your job, do you regularly come into contact with whites?
Yes _____    No _____
Do you consider any of these white workers to be:
A close friend that you can talk over confidential matters with
Yes _____    No _____
A good friend to whom you can say what you really think
Yes _____    No _____
Someone who calls you by your first name
Yes _____    No _____
Someone you just know to speak to
Yes _____    No _____

Has the company done anything special to improve opportunities for Negro workers?

IF YES:
What have they done?  (Full details)
Why have they done this?  (PROBE)

Has the company done anything special to bring job openings to the attention of Negroes?

IF YES:
What have they done?
Why have they done this?
How do most Negro job-seekers find out about openings in this company?

How much of an effort do you think the top management of this company is making to improve opportunities for Negro workers in this company?  (Why do you feel this way?)

How about your immediate supervisor? How interested do you think he is in improving opportunities for Negro workers in this company?

> Why do you feel this way? (Record any incidents that indicate positive or negative actions on the part of the supervisor.)

Are there one or two people in this company who have taken the lead in trying to improve opportunities for the Negro worker?

IF YES:
Who are they?
Why are they doing this?
What have they been doing?

## SCHEDULE V

## UNION QUESTIONNAIRE

How do you personally feel about this policy? (Probe)
Are there others in the union who feel differently? (IF YES: Who are these people? How do they feel about the policy?)

To what extent was the union involved in the planning and development of this policy?
Can you tell me a little about that?

Has the company policy on equal employment opportunity caused any special problems for the union?

IF YES:
Can you tell me about them?
Have these problems been solved, or are they still present?

IF SOLVED:
Can you tell me how these problems were dealt with?

What part, if any, is played by the union in the company's equal employment opportunity program? (Probe for details.)
Has the company and the union worked together on any project to improve equal employment opportunities? (IF YES: Can you give me the details?)

What is the size of your local?
Approximately what proportion are Negroes?
Approximately in what year did your union get its first Negro member?

Has a Negro ever served as an official in this union?
    (IF YES:   Have Negroes ever been stewards? IF YES: About how many?)  What is the highest job held by a Negro in the union?

# ABOUT THE AUTHOR

Louis A. Ferman is an Associate Professor in the School of Social Work at the University of Michigan and is also Research Director of the Institute of Labor and Industrial Relations, sponsored jointly by the University of Michigan and Wayne State University. His long interest in social problems has resulted in research studies (principally for the Institute of Labor and Industrial Relations) into such fields as plant shutdowns, mental health of unemployed workers, job dislocations, and integration. He has been a member of the teaching staffs on social research, social problems, and industrial sociology at Wayne State University and Oakland University.

Mr. Ferman's articles on social problems have appeared in various journals, and he has co-authored a number of books, including Poverty in America, Negroes and Jobs: A Reader, Economic Failure and Alienation, and Fighting the War on Poverty.

Mr. Ferman studied at Brown and Boston Universities and received his Ph.D. degree from Cornell University.